THE SÁMI PEOPLE –
TRADITIONS IN TRANSITION

In appreciation
dedicated to

Áillohaš
Nils-Aslak Valkeapää

in memoriam
1943-2001

THE SÁMI PEOPLE

TRADITIONS IN TRANSITION

Veli-Pekka Lehtola

translated by
Linna Weber Müller-Wille

UNIVERSITY OF ALASKA PRESS · FAIRBANKS

Fourth Printing
Revised second edition © 2004 Veli-Pekka Lehtola

North American edition published and distributed by:

University of Alaska Press
P.O. Box 756240
Fairbanks, AK 99775
888.252.6657
fypress@uaf.edu
www.uaf.edu/uapress

Printed in the United States of America

Library of Congress Cataloging-in-Publication Data on file

ISBN 10: 1-889963-75-5
ISBN 13: 978-1-889963-75-4

Translated from the revised Finnish edition:

Saamelaiset: Historia, Yhteiskunta, Taide [The Sámi: History, Society, Art]. Jyväskylä, Finland: Kustannus-Puntsi, 1997. ISBN 951-97541-2-1.

Linna Weber Müller-Wille, translator
Heather Dawn, editor and proofreader
Ragnar Müller-Wille, editor and proofreader
Ludger Müller-Wille, scientific consulting
Petteri Lehtinen, cover designer

Translation was supported by the Finnish Literature Information Center. Production and printing of the original Finnish edition was supported by the Thule Institute and Giellagas Institute (University of Oulu) and the Sámi Information Center (Arctic Center, Rovaniemi).

Cover photographs:

top: Ieš Pieti or Per-Anders Vasara (here with his wife Kristiina) was a Sámi preacher who spread Laestadianism at the end of the 1900s. Collage by Jaakko Heikkilä.
center: Parade of the City Sámi carrying the Sámi flag on National Day in Helsinki, February 6, 1993. Photo by Jorma Lehtola.
bottom: In artistic handicraft, old designs unite with new perceptions. *Solju*, a woman's brooch made by Petteri Laiti, silversmith from Aanaar. Photo by Petteri Laiti.

Back cover photograph:

Veli-Pekka Lehtola poses with a painting by Merja Aletta Ranttila. Photograph by Jorma Lehtola.

PREFACE

The Sámi, undoubtedly, are the most studied people in Europe, if not the world. The centres of western civilization, be it in Rome through Tacitus, in England through Ottar, in Sweden through Olaus Magnus, or in Central Europe through Johannes Scheffer - to mention a few - have felt an indescribable attraction to go beyond their reach seeking revelations about peoples - the Sámi - and places - Ultima Thule - at the edge of the magic North.

Such works have shaped the external images of the Sámi in Sápmi, their lands in northernmost Europe. These descriptions of Sámi culture, society, language and livelihood became a lasting external representation of the Sámi which was maintained, rightly or wrongly, through the power of print as texts, maps and drawings.

The Sámi points of view and interpretations of their own culture and history seldom emerged through these texts in foreign languages. Furthermore, these treatises often expressed the futility of the continuation of the Sámi people as a distinct culture and nation being gradually integrated into modern western nation-states. Would there be then a future for this aboriginal nation?

Today, at the beginning of the 21st century, such presumptuous predictions have been disproved. Sámi, living now in Sápmi, on the Finnish, Norwegian, Swedish and Russian sides and being dispersed outside their own area, have continuously shown adaptation to changing human and environmental conditions. Their statements of a distinct cultural and regional identity - people and land - are vibrant. For some time, Sámi writers, artists, philosophers and scientists have made contributions to provide their own people as well as neighbouring peoples with interpretations of their own heritage and knowledge in either Sámi or foreign languages.

Veli-Pekka Lehtola, a Sámi from Aanaar (Anár) in Sápmi, on the Finnish side, is one of the generation of Sámi scientists who has tackled the task of Sámi representation versus the deluge of external studies. His research into life histories, literary analysis of both Sámi and Finnish writers, Sámi artists, and the Sámi-Finnish culture contact has been meticulous, careful and highly convincing.

This book is not a monograph dealing with ethnography, regional geography, or history. Rather, in a refined way, Veli-Pekka Lehtola weaves an historical and contemporary picture of the Sámi and Sápmi by presenting aspects and events that are characteristic of Sámi traditions in transitions. By transitions he means the internal and external developments and climaxes that have shaped Sámi culture and society as Sámi express their voices today in multifaceted ways within the context of continuous contact with neighbouring societies who have the majority and power.

Veli-Pekka Lehtola, who holds a doctorate in literature studies from the University of Oulu (Finland) and is a lecturer in aboriginal and northern cultures in the Giellagas Institute at the same institution, has succeeded in a very succinct manner to provide the English reading world with a comprehensive insight into Sámi history and contemporary expressions and thinking. His treatise is a most welcome addition to the growing number of texts published by Sámi themselves in various languages.

It is crucial that the Sámi points of view are fully expressed and respected based on solid presentations of facts and their interpretation. In Veli-Pekka Lehtola's own words, the intentions of his book are " ... to build bridges of knowledge among cultures."

Professor Ludger Müller-Wille
McGill University
Montréal (Québec) Canada, 1 August 2002

TRANSLATOR´S NOTE

The main goal of the translation of this book was to bring the reader into the Sámi perspective, giving an inside experience of Sámi culture and history. One way to do this was to use *Sápmi*, the homeland of the Sámi people, whenever their territory is mentioned, even as it changed through time and history, and to use Sámi place names. Many of them are official names that are used side by side with other official names, as a result of language laws. A glossary was added that includes the equivalents in the other official languages. Still, on maps the curious reader will see other versions, but will at least have an awareness that these Sámi place names are the most ancient, and are a part of Sámi identity.

Sámi Atlas (1996) by Hans Ragnar Mathisen, Samuli Aikio and Anders Henriksen is an excellent reference, easy to use by non-Sámi. It would be a handy companion to use while reading this present book, to visualize both historical and present, areas and places, siida territories, Treaties, boundaries and more that Veli-Pekka Lehtola discusses.

Here and there other words from a Sámi language appear with a brief explanation the first time they are used. In this way words like *noaidi*, *duodji* and *Sámediggi* become a part of the regular language and experience of the reader.

Many different spellings of Sámi have been used over the years in texts written by non-Sámi and Sámi, alike. For a long time the spelling of Sámi was not standardized. The author and I have chosen to use *Sámi*, their own name for themselves as it is written in their own language, and encourage others to use it too, for the following reasons:

- English is very good at accepting words from all languages and therefore it is best to use the spelling *Sámi* the way the Sámi do. Accents and other signs are also routinely and commonly used for personal names and loan words, for example Bartók, Chloé, Noël, déjà vu.

- Using the original taken directly from Sámi also shows respect.

- People assume, in general, that accents are not to be used in English. This is false. They are optional and are used to indicate particular emphasis of pronunciation that the writer wishes. Example: learned and learnèd. In this case not only the pronunciation is changed but also the meaning.

- Keeping the accent immediately lets a reader know that the sound must be different from any English sound, short or long, and signals the reader to be aware that they should find out how it is pronounced, and make the best approximation.

- Often the versions *Saami* or *Same* have been used. Very few words in English have *aa*, most of them loan words like aardvark, and the pronunciation is arbitrary. It would usually be spoken as a long English *a* as in ape, age, same - not at all like what it should be for Sámi. This certainly applies to the sometimes used version *Same* - the Sámi are certainly not the *same* as any other people!

In any translation, idioms and phrasing are often nearly impossible to convey to speakers of another language. I tried to reflect the actual content and emotional feel of the text for a deeper understanding.

Linna Weber Müller-Wille
St. Lambert (Québec) Canada, August 2002

LIST OF CONTENTS

Photo from the *Kadja-Nilla* series by the Sámi photographer Marja Helander. Kadja-Nilla was one of the last large reindeer owners from Deatnu at the beginning of the 1900s.

MULTIFACETED SÁPMI

Sámi culture has changed greatly in recent decades. Since the 1970s, Sámi identity has developed in a new direction in response to new influences and viewpoints. In the last decade, Sápmi, the Sámi homeland, has become a symbol of identity for the Sámi people - it represents Sámi unity in the modern world. Representatives from Sápmi attend official conferences of aboriginal peoples all over the world.

The four-coloured Sámi flag flies at conferences and meetings. The national anthem, written by Isak Saba in the beginning of the 20th century, has had a revival and even competes with the new "folk yoiks". These celebrate great Sámi events and notable Sámi personages, who are being rediscovered. There are seven official flag days. The national day on February 6th commemorates the first meeting in 1917 of Sámi from all the Nordic countries.

The expression of Sámi identity, revealed in the form of symbols, is a result of the "awakening" of the Sámi people over the course of the last quarter century. In the early 1970s, young Sámi, reacting against a long process of assimilation, began to become aware of Sámi heritage and to fight for it. World War II, the rebuilding after the war, the construction of roads and communications networks, changing customs and education all took place within the ideals and values of the dominant societies in Finland, Norway, Sweden and Russia.

From the beginning, the main aim of young educated Sámi was to build a bridge between tradition and modern times; between old lifestyles and the influences of modern society. New modes of participation quickly came into being: new forms of Sámi politics, media and art. The most important turning point in Sámi political and cultural history was the Áltá Conflict, a movement in the early 1980s, which spoke out against a hydro-electric dam proposed for the Áltá River. This gave impetus to Sámi culture and resulted in important changes in Sámi politics in Norway, and inspired a whole generation of Sámi throughout Sápmi.

Incorporating foreign influences is not new to the Sámi - dialogue between the old and the modern is an age-old tradition. They have always lived in the borderlands between cultures and influences. Artist and world citizen Nils-Aslak Valkeapää portrayed in his art his own background of living on the borders between several states and cultures. His background gave rise to his desire and inclination to overcome the borders through art and through cultural and political activism. In Valkeapää's words the question is not about "internationalism" but about a natural way of living. Overcoming borders creates new avenues, but also tensions, without which there is no progress. "The only genuine thing is just what lives", Valkeapää declared.

New laws and Sámi political awareness have raised the appreciation of Sámi culture, but on a daily level the situation is still not without controversy. Because Sámi culture is spread among four countries, it is not protected by strong and clear borders. The status of the Sámi languages still needs to be strengthened. Increased efforts of assimilation by the States after World War II left many Sámi with poor self esteem, which still causes them problems, for instance, in their relationship to Sámi language.

A people divided by borders

The Sámi are the only ethnic group in the European Union to be recognized as an aboriginal people. They are a minority living in four countries and have their own language and culture. Sámi number between 60,000 and 100,000, depending on how they are counted. Sápmi extends from central Norway and Sweden and across northern Finland and the Kola Peninsula in Russia.

The largest population of Sámi, 40 - 50,000, live in Norway, half of these in the province of Finnmark. In Sweden there are 15 - 25,000 Sámi, in Finland at least 7000 and in Russia about 2000. Sámi in Finland, Sweden and Norway elect representatives from amongst themselves to their respective Sámediggi, Sámi Parliament which has advisory powers to the State governments.

In Finland, Norway and Sweden a Sámi is defined as a person of Sámi origin who feels oneself to be Sámi and who either has Sámi as their first language or has at least one parent or grandparent who had Sámi as their first language. In Russia a Sámi is defined by self-ascription. What is important is ancestry, relationship to the Sámi language and through that to Sámi culture and a feeling of being Sámi.

More than half of the Sámi speak Sámi. There are actually several Sámi languages and Sámi from the different language groups usually cannot understand each other. North Sámi is the principal language in Finland, Norway and Sweden. Finland and Norway have language laws guaranteeing Sámi the right to use their own language with authorities.

The name Sámi (sápmelaš) is an ethnic designation signifying that Sámi view themselves as members of a culture set apart from the dominant cultures. It supplants the term "Lapp" which was given by outsiders. In the beginning "Lapp" meant people who lived on the periphery and were not farmers and therefore were uncivilized. It came to be a derogatory term and should no longer be used. It should also not be confused with "Laplander". Laplanders are people who live in the province of Lapland in Finland, regardless of whether they are Sámi or Finns.

Outsiders also used other names when writing about the Sámi. In the very earliest written sources the words "Fenni", "Finn", usually meant a Sámi person. The term "Lapp" in documents and literature was used from about the 12th century to designate a person who practised "Lappish" economic activities - fishing and hunting and later reindeer herding - in an area that they permanently owned and for which they paid property tax to the State.

The word Sámi used by majorities (same, samisk in Scandinavian languages and saamelainen in Finnish, and in Russian saamskii) is of fairly recent occurrence, coming into use only in the early 1900s in literature written in the majority languages. The term sápmelaš only began appearing in writings when the Sámi themselves became literate and started writing. This Sámi word derives from an age-old Finno-Ugrian word, from which the Finnish name for themselves as a cultural group, suomalainen, also derives.

Diversity of the Sámi people

New modes of participation are accompanied by the need to reexamine old ideas of Sámi and their emerging ethnic, national identity - of self-image. Up until now the original Sámi culture has been seen as depending mainly on traditional livelihoods, lifestyles and cultural models. In the eyes of outsiders "true" Sámi have been only those who live in nature and are uncivilized. In the changing circumstances many older concepts are being reexamined.

In historic literature about Sámi many names have been used: Forest Lapp, Reindeer Sámi, River Lapp, Eastern Sámi, etc. Classifications are useful for understanding the basis of Sámi culture. However, they can be bewildering and must not be confused. Linguistic, geographic, ecologic, historic and economic classifications do not concur. It must also be remembered that, since the postwar era, some of the divisions have become outdated because circumstances have changed and former traits have become blended. The significance of traditional livelihoods has diminished noticeably while commercial and service occupations have increased.

A quite common idea is that all Sámi have always been, and still are, reindeer herders - Reindeer or Mountain Sámi. In reality, for example, in Finland only one in every five owns reindeer and not all of them have reindeer herding as their main livelihood. Reindeer herding has been an emblem of the whole culture even though that economic sector is historically rather recent, only "just" beginning in the 1500s.

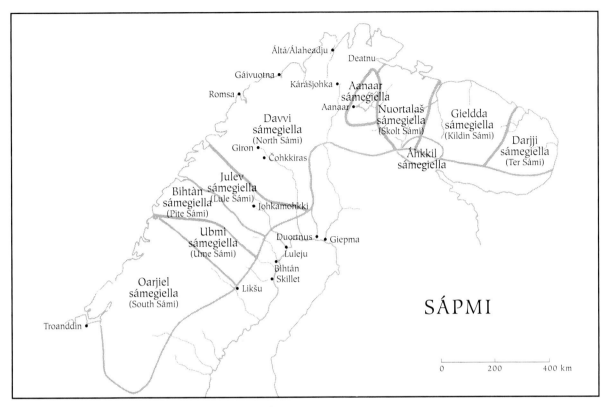

SÁMI LANGUAGES

The Sámi languages belong to the Finno-Ugrian language family. That means that Sámi is related to Finnish, not to the Scandinavian languages and not to Russian or any Indo-European language. The current thinking is that Sámi and Finnish forebearers spoke a common language 3000-4000 years ago. Their livelihoods and cultures took different directions and developed different characteristics.

Proto-Sámi then split into dialects that eventually became the Sámi languages spoken today. Because of the great expanse of the area, groups became isolated from one another and followed different livelihoods. Across the millennia the Sámi languages borrowed words from other languages, such as from the Baltic and the Germanic language groups, from Finnish, and from the Scandinavian languages and Russian.

Differences between some languages became so great that speakers of the different Sámi languages cannot understand each other. In spite of all these different influences it is still possible to recognize the original base of the languages through their common structure, for instance in the similarities of place names throughout Sápmi.

Today about 50,000 people speak a Sámi language, the majority speak North Sámi. The language boundaries do not correspond to the State borders, most of which were drawn in the last few hundred years. Ten Sámi languages are distinguished, separated into two main groups: Western and Eastern Sámi. To the western group belong the North, Lule, Pite, Ume, and South Sámi

languages; to the eastern group belong Aanaar, Skolt, Akkala, Kildin and Ter Sámi. It should be noted that each group simply called their respective language *Sámi* (in various forms). The names for the different languages were given by linguists. The Sámi have now adapted these names into official use: Davvi-, Julevu-, Bihtán-, Ubmi- and Oarjielsámegiella; Aanaar-, Nuortalaš-, Áhkkil-, Gieldda- and Darjjisámegiella.

North Sámi has the most speakers; about 17,000, of whom 10,000 live in Norway, 5000 in Sweden and 2000 in Finland. Lule Sámi is spoken by about 3000 people, Kildin by about 650, Aanaar and Skolt by 300 to 500 each, and the others by very few. Áhkkil is no longer a living language. The main languages are again divided into dialects.

Almost every main language has its own orthography or way of spelling. In the 1600s and 1700s literature was usually written in the Ume and Lule languages. For the largest language, North Sámi, written language really began to develop in the 1800s. Within North Sámi several writing standards have been used that were different in Norway, Sweden and Finland during most of the 20th century. In 1979 all three countries adopted a single standard orthography for North Sámi.

The present writing standard for Aanaar Sámi took shape one hundred years ago. In contrast, the first Skolt Sámi book with new orthography was published only in 1972. In Russia, as they were in Soviet times, books in Eastern Sámi languages are published in Cyrillic letters.

It may seem surprising that the Sea Sámi living on the shores of the Arctic Ocean make up the largest group - nearly half. Reindeer herding is a very small part of their lifestyle. The Sea Sámi live only in Norway. Their language is one of the dialects of North Sámi.

Taking the area where Sámi live in Finland as an example, there are four Sámi groups distinguished by economic and cultural differences. The oldest settled group are the Lake Aanaar (Anár) Sámi whose livelihood has been based on a mixed economy of freshwater fishing and small scale farming. Some Deatnu Sámi have the same type of livelihood, but with the addition of reindeer herding. Some Deatnu Sámi today own farmsteads and live from dairy agriculture, and raise cattle or sheep.

The Reindeer Sámi, who live in the regions of Eanodat, Giehtaruohtas and Soabbat, used extensive areas in the fells until the end of the 1800s when the closing of the State borders forced them to settle in a smaller area. The Skolt Sámi today live in Čeavetjávri and Nellim (Njellim, Njeä'llem), settlements that were built after World War II for their resettlement from the Petsamo (Peäccam) area which was ceded to the Soviet Union.

Historical documents mention Forest Sámi, an older culture than Reindeer Sámi. They followed a livelihood based on a closeness to nature and a diverse economy of hunting, fishing and gathering and, later, small scale reindeer herding. The Forest Sámi Culture extended from the coniferous forest belt of central Scandinavia to the forest and lake areas of the Kola Peninsula.

Another important classification is based on language. There are nine Sámi languages spoken today, some of which have more than one dialect. These are truly different languages that evolved from the Proto-Sámi root language over the past thousand years. They are so different that a North Sámi speaker can only understand Skolt Sámi or Aanaar Sámi with great difficulty.

The language group with the widest distribution is North Sámi. It is spoken in the Deatnu area, the Guovdageaidnu and Eanodat regions, and in northern Sweden. It is the language with the largest body of literature, although others are also written languages - South, Lule, Aanaar, Skolt and Kildin Sámi. Three main languages are represented in Finland with speakers of Aanaar, Skolt and North Sámi. In Norway and Sweden South, Ume, Pite, Lule and North Sámi are spoken; in Russia Kildin, Ter and Skolt.

The language of clothing

People often speak of Sámi culture, Sámi attire and Sámi language as if there were one unchanging, uniform people. It is often forgotten that Sápmi is very diverse, both economically and culturally. During the course of their history Sámi moved into many places where they developed different cultural traits.

One of the most distinct symbols is the Sámi garment. When Sámi gather together from distant places the surest way of recognizing each one's home is to look at their clothing. The design and decoration of the clothing differ for each place. From the general distinguishing features of the garment a Sámi traditionally identifies the other's home area and, from subtle differences, even their home village and family.

To take Finland as an example, there are five main designs among the 7000 Finnish Sámi living in the municipalities of Eanodat, Anár (Aanaar) and Ohcejohka and the northern portion of Soadegilli. The most well-known is the Mountain Sámi garment, the "Eanodat style", which has been a favourite for postcards and tourist pictures because of the colourful men's tunic. It is decorated with many embroidered ribands sewn onto the shoulders and hem, as well as on the high hat that crowns the outfit. The lavish adornments of the brooch worn on the breast as well as on the fine belts became widespread after the war. The garment became a measure of wealth; its material, colours, ornamentation and the number of brooches indicate social standing.

In contrast is the "Ohcejohka style" which is simpler and less extravagant. The men's tunic has one yellow and several red strips on the shoulders; on the hem there is nothing. The hem on the women's skirt is a ruffle of red wool. People from Ohcejohka laugh about the "Anár (Aanaar) style" men's tunic because it differs from the one in Ohcejohka by having an orange ruffled hem that is "like a woman's".

12

The garment of the Skolt Sámi man has adopted influences from other Sámi groups' dress during the last decades. The woman's headdress is determined by her marital status.

The Soabbat garment. The man wears the traditional Four Wind hat. Sámi women often use their own hat, although they otherwise dress in modern European fashions.

SÁMI GARMENTS
ON THE FINNISH SIDE

The Aanaar (left) and the Eanodat tunic decoration became considerably more elaborate after the war. Photo: Jorma Lehtola.

The Ohcejohka or Deatnu garment is less extravagantly decorated. It is used throughout the Deatnu region. Photos: Toivo Kauppinen.

The fourth design is the "Skolt style", which is very different from all the others. The women's dress is similar to the women's Finnish folk costume from Karelia. The "horn" hat that has disappeared everywhere else in Sápmi has been preserved as the Skolt Sámi women's headdress.

The fifth design is the "Vuohčču style" from the Soabbat region. It is similar to the colourful Anár (Aanaar) attire, but the women's hat is decorated in the Eanodat style with fewer colourful ribbons.

The clothing tells many things. Even a person's character traits can be discerned from the way it is worn. Is the hat worn correctly, are the reindeer fur shoes carefully bound, is the brooch straight and the tunic worn right? All of these things have always been particular. Especially in earlier days, at church gatherings or at the markets, the way a person dressed was always observed. The worst thing that could be said of a badly dressed woman was that she was a *rivgu* (not a Sámi).

The garment is a symbol of a Sámi person's identity. It has many subtleties that are difficult to describe, and that contain Sámi cultural vocabulary and codes, just like shades of meaning in the language. It also reveals an unaccustomed wearer or someone from outside. For that reason many Sámi resent or even become angry at outsiders who wear Sámi clothing without understanding its symbolic language.

Unfortunately this happens often in tourist activities, especially in northern Finland. Outsiders do not generally know how to wear Sámi clothing in the proper manner. Sometimes people mix different dress styles, even men's and women's clothes. All of these kinds of attitudes show an indifference for Sámi cultural traditions.

The language - a map of reality

For decades the Sámi language has been submersed under the majority language of each country: Finnish, Norwegian, Swedish, Russian. Those are the languages used in the schools, public offices, media. That is now changing. Appreciation of Sámi is increasing. Sámi media have revived the language; words and expressions that were on the verge of disappearing have again come into use and new words are being coined. Sámi is taught both as mother tongue and as a second language. Knowledge and use of Sámi is spreading.

The issue is not just about language alone. Nils-Aslak Valkeapää said, "People who only know one language think that in another language the words are only replaced with equivalent ones. It probably never even occurs to them that the whole way of thinking may be different and that things may be seen in a different way."

Language is not just a means of communicating information, it also contains the central cultural elements of a people. This has been underlined by a number of linguists at Nordic universities.

Ethnologist Israel Ruong said that language is the map of Sámi reality. It may also open to others the way to a comprehensive view of Sámi culture. Human language reflects its usage. Expressions are developed as they are needed, especially in areas that are important. There is a saying that people from the Deatnu River speak of *luossa* (salmon) by many different names, but other fish are just *guolit* (fish). Of course, the saying is not the complete truth, but it does give the picture.

Each language has its own particular fields with especially rich vocabularies. In Sámi these have to do with nature and reindeer. T. I. Itkonen listed over 500 expressions relating to reindeer in his catalogue of vocabulary in the Finnish part of Sápmi. Reindeer are differentiated by colour, age and antler shape, for instance. According to Pekka Sammallahti, naming reindeer draws upon some hundred roots and stems to build countless variants to distinguish every single reindeer.

The Sámi language is also particularly precise for describing the qualities of natural phenomena and places. Nils Jernsletten listed hundreds of words in Sámi relating to snow and ice. The vocabulary denoting the different characteristics of snow is so precise that it is now being used as a base for developing a terminology for international scientific use.

Leif Rantala counted the words describing landscape in one dictionary. There were 109 words depicting shapes of mountains and hills; 40 for bogs and marshes; and 60 for valleys, ravines and hollows. For example *vággi* is a "shortish, deepish valley"; *gorsa* is a "smallish, deep ravine"; *gurra* is a "ravine, gorge, narrow valley"; *roggi* a "pit"; *lákku* a "flat highland valley"; and *leakši* is an "ordinary marshy, widish valley on a treeless mountain".

To express a single Sámi word in other languages many words, or even whole sentences, must be used. That is why some northern Finnish dialects borrowed many Sámi words describing topography since equivalent words did not exist in Finnish.

Also the vocabulary depicting human activities is very exact, according to Sammallahti. Human and animal activities are differentiated. For example, for a person and a dog the same word cannot be used to mean "lies down": the person *veallá*; the dog *goarjada*. Even dogs have special status - other animals *livvadit*. Sámi can easily describe hundreds of motions. Does someone laugh long or short, broadly or with puckered lips, with shaking sides or dryly? That will determine which word is to be used.

These are all examples of the richness of the language - it is irreplaceable. Kerttu Vuolab, a Sámi writer, has emphasized the significance of a small language as a medium for transmitting life experiences and a particular environment. That is why all languages are equally valuable. Just as every culture is unique in its way of adapting to its living environment, small languages are just as valuable as "languages spoken by billions" in preserving guidelines for living.

Vuolab says, "Even a language spoken by billions is only one language; it is like a school of herring all swimming in the same direction. The language of a small people is like a fox pup unprotected by the pack. It must watch and listen to avoid danger, it looks around and takes note of others. The dominant populations, which are losing touch with guidelines for survival, could learn much from the fox pup."

The Reindeer Sámi settlement Bálojávri in Eanodat from the 1930s to the 1970s. In 1934 Paavo Ravila took a picture of Matti Palojärvi's family in front of their house (top). In the 1960s Kalle Kuittinen gathered Matti's descendants in the same place (centre). The house was altered to the fashion of the 1970s when the residential heating system was improved by state subsidies or the "heating penny" during the Energy Crisis (bottom).

FROM TACITUS TO LAPPOLOGISTS

Few peoples in the world have been portrayed so often in literature as the Sámi (called "Lapps" in earlier writings). Often the authors' own cultural and social background influenced the portrayal of the Sámi's real circumstances. These old portrayals of "Lapps" can be interpreted as literary works, in which motives, structure and themes can be distinguished that reflect the point of view of the writer.

The Lapland and "Lappish" culture of literature are concepts that have their own history and tradition of images and vocabulary. Their existence is largely based on satisfying "Southern" readers. The portrayal has been handed down from one text to another, and has resulted in a discrepancy between the texts and reality.

Myths and truths

From the beginning, reality and myths were mixed and accumulated in literature about "Lapps". Indeed, toward the end of the first century, Tacitus' portrayal in *Germania* was a collection of clichés that writers of the time used to depict "wild" or "primitive" peoples. What was new in his portrayal was, for example, the idea that women took part in hunting alongside men.

Later writers added new details to the picture: Sámi lived in regions where the sun did not set at night; they were skiers, *scritifinoi*; they were powerful sorcerers. These reinforced the previous portrayals. Certain myths, often particularly strange ideas, were repeated in one book after another, sustaining the picture. True observations were often

wrongly interpreted and thus became myths that led to new myths.

In the mid 1500s Olaus Magnus published his *Historia de gentibus septentrionalis* (A History of Northern Peoples), bringing forth a new, even revolutionary, flood of information on Lapland. Unlike his predecessors, Olaus Magnus based his portrayal partly on his own experiences from his travels as far north as Torneå. Magnus' book contains many topics that awakened and directed interest in Lapland during the centuries that followed: midnight sun, cold winters, "Laplanders'" friendliness, hospitality and decency, the lively trade at Torneå, and salmon fishing on the Torneå River.

Magnus' clear portrayal of Sámi shamanism influenced Joannis Schefferus' classic work *Lapponia*, which was published in 1673. An even greater impetus for his book is connected with the wars in which Sweden was involved as a world power during the 1600s. Sweden's enemies propagated vicious rumours that the Swedes would use Sámi sorcerers to assure victory. The Swedish crown, therefore, ordered Schefferus to correct this idea in a book giving a truthful picture of the Sámi people.

Lapponia was the first monograph to focus on the Sámi and as such it clearly belongs to the realm of scholarly thinking. Although Schefferus continued the discussion handed down from Antiquity and views inherited from the Middle Ages, he was able to examine in an organized and rational way the various characteristics of Sámi culture. For example, he was a pioneer in his views on history, Sámi

language and mythology. The portrayals in his book were based on the ones made by clergymen living among the Sámi.

From the 1600s ever more researchers, administrators and travellers visited Lapland. Besides working or travelling, they wrote down their experiences and observations. The earliest visitors were merchants and missionaries. Curiosity and the search for the exotic also attracted people to Lapland, and later the prospects of using the natural resources of the North, which was stimulated by scientific inquiry.

Explorers and scientists

By the end of the 1700s literature on Lapland had swelled to a flood. Actual travel literature increased during the 1700s because of the Enlightenment, and especially Romanticism, when many foreign travellers visited Lapland to see Europe's remote periphery and its exotic "people of nature". These books were written purely from an outsider's point of view.

The other main genre of literature on Lapland, written in Swedish, contained presentations (*relationer*) and descriptions (*beskrifningar*) by civil servants (bureaucrats, scientists, surveyors, etc.) who were sent by the Swedish Crown to live in Lapland. These were often written by clergymen, who formed the first educated class in Lapland. They were preachers trained in the use of words to formulate sermons. Their activities in natural sciences or social activities stemmed from a need to keep them in their memory. The writings of these "experts" were often systematically structured.

Both of these types in their own way carried on the tradition of the older portrayals of Lapland. They were a combination of personal experiences, common beliefs, and influences from literature. By going through all the noteworthy literature before their departure and after their trip, travellers learned what had been said about Lapland. For that reason, even portrayals based on personal experiences always related back to previous literature. Sámi were portrayed as representing a different kind of culture.

Starting with Olaus Magnus, outsiders became interested in the northernmost strongholds of civilization as well as the appearance of agriculture at the frontier. As settlement spread vigorously northward in the 1700s, the picture of Lapland changed and had a strong influence until the 1900s. Agriculture began to be emphasized and set as a contrast to Sámi culture. Experts speculated at great length on the economic conditions of Lapland, but travellers also began to point out the importance that agriculture could have as an economic basis for livelihood even in Lapland.

Farming culture had gained a foothold in the wild lands. Those who had conquered the border-lands represented outposts of civilization in a hostile land. Finnish peasants, who struggled valiantly against conditions north of the Arctic Circle, were clearly idealized in portrayals, for example by Joseph Marshall and Giuseppe Acerbi, and others in the 1800s. The idealization of the peasantry by professionals, travellers and local authorities began to blindly focus exclusively on agriculture as the salvation for the northern areas, although it often proved to be a poor alternative.

A "Mountain Sámi *goahti*" in Giuseppe Acerbi's travel book (1802).

In the 1800s most portrayals from professional writings were of a more scientific nature, and the mysticism surrounding Sámi began to disappear. Nevertheless, most of the myths persisted, such as the idea of the naive aboriginal and poor but happy primitive folk. These new works emphasized the contrast between people in a "natural state" and "developed" culture.

This was particularly evident in the theory of race that the social-darwinists projected onto culture. Sámi culture was deemed "lower" and "more primitive" than agricultural cultures. The theory of race flourished in Scandinavia after the mid 1800s, but was caught in controversy early in the 1900s.

Leading scientists such as J. K. Qvigstad in Norway, K. B. Wiklund in Sweden and T. I. Itkonen in Finland studied the languages and ethnography in addition to Sámi history. These "Lappologists" collected detailed and comprehensive information on Sámi.

Nevertheless these researchers' own darwinist and political leanings coloured their supposedly "objective" works. For example, Wiklund's proposed "Lappish" school system was based on the idea that "A Lapp must remain a Lapp", the backdrop conveying the image of Sámi as a weaker culture that degenerates because of contact with a "higher" culture.

In the 1900s fiction and prose began to depict Sámi more often. For writers, Sámi represented mystical and primitive strength that should be tamed by Christianity, Peasantry and Civilization.

"Ieš Pieti" or Per-Anders Vasara (here with his wife Kristiina) was a Sámi preacher spreading Laestadianism at the end of the 1900s. Collage: Jaakko Heikkilä.

MILESTONES OF SÁMI HISTORY

There is a widespread idea that Sámi culture has remained unchanged through thousands of years. Even recent local histories present the image of "Lapps" in their four-cornered hats wandering the countryside with their reindeer herds thousands of years ago. The truth is that the four-cornered hat as well as the present method of reindeer herding were developed much later. Sámi prehistory is a series of continuous crises which produced changes that greatly influenced the overall aspects of their culture.

Sámi had to meet the challenges of adapting to the pressures of changing circumstances and culture. Nature determined the setting for their way of life. The organization of yearly cycles - migrating with the seasons from one environment to another - was the most effective way to take advantage of an austere nature. From time to time they had to change their livelihood to meet crises in nature, and then the culture changed too.

The Sámi have lived among many peoples in northern Europe. Their culture was not so isolated as is often supposed. The presence of other populations and cultures constantly offered new influences, challenges and pressures for change. The Sámi have dynamically assimilated influences, taking some parts permanently into their own culture. They have adapted even to great changes without losing their own identity as Sámi.

The settlement of Fennoscandia

People began to arrive in Fennoscandia around 11,000 - 10,000 BC as the ice of the glaciers that covered the area for tens of thousands of years gradually melted. The glacier reached its greatest extent in the area of what is now Central Europe and Central Russia. At its southern edge, peoples who lived by hunting wild reindeer and elk (moose) began to spread northward as land that was suitable for the game animals became ice-free. Researchers nowadays are careful not to talk about settlers coming either from the west or the east. It is a complicated picture of spreading cultural complexes with central traits that were shaped by influences from both west and east. The flood of settlement followed two directions: one northward toward the shores of the Arctic Ocean, the other came from the East heading toward the area that is now Finland.

Cultural zones developed very early on and were characteristic of later periods as well. On the shores of the Arctic Ocean, the Komsa Culture held sway from Murmansk Fjord to the Romsa (Tromsa) region. Farther south, the Fosna Culture was located in the area between where Bergen and Oslo are today. The Suomusjärvi Culture was found in the middle part of present day Finland, and the Onega region to the east seems to have developed its own cultural sphere.

Earlier, it was assumed that there were large unsettled areas that isolated the cultural groups from each other. Modern archaeological research has shown, to the contrary, that, already during the thousands of years immediately following the ice age, there was settlement throughout the area of present day Finland. Even on the Kola Peninsula and in northern Sweden so many Stone Age settlement sites have been found that one may presume that all of Fennoscandia was thinly but evenly populated already then.

We can only form a sketchy picture of the life of those northern Stone Age people. Archaeological finds lack organic materials. Objects and dwellings were made of materials that decompose: bone, antler, leather and wood. Rock carvings and miniature art from the Stone Age have been preserved to the present. These, along with cliff drawings and items made of amber, project a limited picture of the world of these Stone Age peoples, their thoughts and ideas, from thousands of years ago. The northern European hunting art tradition lasted from the end of the youngest Stone Age, or Neolithic, (the beginning of the Finno-Ugrian influence) to the end of the Bronze Age (around 4000 to 500 BC).

The most important collection of rock art is found in northern Norway, mainly in the Áltá area, and in the east in Karelia and on the Kola Peninsula. Typical themes in the rock art are hunting, fishing, animals and rituals. There are no themes depicting domestic work or homesteading, handicrafts or production. That is also characteristic of the later art of noaidi drums. Rock art is mainly found along the banks of water bodies and is probably related to nearby settlements used seasonally during annual migration.

The question of Sámi origins

Sámi origin has always interested researchers because of the unique character of Sámi culture. The image of reindeer herding Sámi has always captured attention as a contrast to the agricultural population of the region. Sámi origins have often been sought in special, imaginative places. Indeed, Sámi "must have" originated in Mongolia or they "must have been" people related to the Nenets, the Komsa culture's direct descendants, or even closely related to the Basques - all of these origins have been claimed.

The basic assumption of such theories has generally been that Sámi became isolated as a population, thus preserving at least some of their original characteristics. The truth, however, is that Sámi are not a particularly uniform group genetically. Also, they were not as isolated as has been supposed. They had lively interaction with other cultures.

In recent decades, the picture from archaeological remains has changed on the basis of more conclusive research from the 1960s onward. The present view of Sámi origins is related to the disproving of the so-called "theory of immigration".

Previously, it had been thought that the main ancestors of the Finno-Ugrian peoples migrated from the Volga by roundabout ways in the second millennium BC or even later, reaching the Finnish peninsula as two distinct peoples, Finns and Sámi.

According to the modern "theory of continuity", there was continuous settlement by Finno-Ugrian peoples in the area that later became Finland, at least since the time of the Comb Ceramic culture of the Stone Age, around six thousand years ago. The main idea is that Finns and Sámi were then not yet separate ethnic groups. The currently prevailing theory is that the Sámi arose as a distinct group from different elements in the region that approximately corresponds to the area of Sámi settlement in the Middle Ages, when they entered the light of modern history. The division of the Finnish-Sámi language was brought about by changes in livelihoods and the resulting changes in ways of life.

Researchers agree that Sámi ethnicity was made distinct when it came into contact with an agricultural population. According to linguists, this happened during the Bronze Age, around the second millennium BC, and probably led to the split of the ancestral language into the Finnish and Sámi language groups. At that time the population of the southwestern and eastern shores of the Finnish landmass were assimilating strong influences from the West. These were brought by new, perhaps rather small, groups of settlers who practiced agriculture - the Battle-axe Culture.

With these influences the population of those shores adopted farming as a new livelihood, while the people living inland retained hunting as the basis for their way of life. This difference in economies pointed the populations in different directions since the groups did not have close interactions with each other. The differentiation of ways of life caused language changes, such that after centuries and millennia the groups no longer could understand one another.

Pressures from Scandinavian and Baltic Sea cultures clearly began to direct the cultural development of the populations in the southwestern part of what is now Finland. While the inland population's relations to the East remained as before, the two populations began to differentiate quickly.

Around 4500 or 5000 years ago, in the coastal

area, the late Comb Ceramic people merged with the Battle-axe people, becoming the Proto-Finnish Culture. From then on the western influence on the Finnish language and gene pool became so great that linguist Pekka Sammallahti has said in jest that "the Finns are Indo-Europeanized Sámi".

The relations of the pre-Sámi population with the eastern influences continued and even dominated. The eastern influence and the assimilation of the inland local traditions into the inland people's sphere developed into the Asbestos Ceramic Culture, which today is seen as ancestral Sámi. Archaeologists have shown that northern Fennoscandia became predominantly Sámi in the first millennium BC.

Norwegian archaeologists have been able to trace distinctive features of the Sámi culture historically from about 800 BC. The main criteria are finds of human skulls in Varanger Fjord. Less clear are features pertaining to ornamentation, use of antler and bone, and possibly reindeer keeping. Likewise, Finnish linguistic research proves that by the beginning of the first millennium BC at the latest, we may speak of a Sámi language as a distinct ethnic trait.

The spread of Sámi in the North Calotte regions is apparently connected to the era of greatest change during the first millennium BC. About half way through that millennium the Comb Ceramic era that was characterized in its last phases by the use of asbestos ceramics ended, as did the occurrence of petroglyphs. There was also a change in the types of dwellings: in place of the earlier pit houses came the *gammi* type, a sod hut, which in later times was the most characteristic dwelling type of the Sámi culture.

The rarity of archaeological artifacts that are found also tells of a change in the way of life. It had become more mobile. This is seen in the dwelling type and in the artifacts becoming lighter. Cumbersome ceramic and metal items disappeared. Organic materials like wood, sod and bone became dominant. Winter dwellings, which in earlier times were massive structures located on the sea shores, were perhaps moved into the mountains where their remains are hard to find. Researchers think, however, that the transition from Bronze Age to Sámi Iron Age was apparently without a break in the cultural continuity.

The Áltá rock paintings appear to present human images of a noaidi or shaman.

Influences from many different directions are typical of Sámi culture. The western influence was particularly strong during the whole prehistoric time on the coast of the Arctic Ocean, at least as far as the southern part of Troms Province. From the East and the Northeast came many influences into Finnmark during the whole Finno-Ugrian era. The boundary of influences was possibly the western border of Kemi Lapland, approximately from the Gulf of Bothnia to Varanger Fjord.

Expansion of the Sámi area

The expanse of the Sámi settlement area was perhaps greatest from around the year 1 to the 11th century AD. Sámi lived from Lake Ladoga to the Arctic Ocean and from central Scandinavia to the White Sea. Except for the southwestern and south-

21

ern coasts, all of the present day area of Finland was Sámi settlement area. The network of small hunting communities used an even larger area. "The siida mosaic" seems to have included all the major water areas.

From the beginning of that era a fur trade apparently began, and hunting for furs became the basis for Sámi livelihood. As Sámi entered into the trade circle of the Romans, their new way of life developed into the Sámi "wilderness supplier" culture, which is reflected in archaeological finds from the Iron Age in a wide Sámi area. It is hardly an accident that the first description of Sámi is in a Roman text. Cornelius Tacitus describes them in his book *Germania*, which appeared in 98 AD.

"In wonderful savageness live the nation of the Fennians (Fenni), and in beastly poverty, destitute of arms, of horses, and of homes; their food, the common herbs; their apparel, skins; their bed, the earth; their only hope in their arrows, which for want of iron they point with bones. Their common support they have from the chase, women as well as men; for with these the former wander up and down, and crave a portion of the prey. Nor other shelter have they even for their babes, against the violence of tempests and ravening beasts, than to cover them with the branches of trees twisted together; this a reception for the old men, and hither resort the young. Such a condition they judge more happy than the painful occupation of cultivating the ground, than the labour of rearing houses, than the agitations of hope and fear attending the defence of their own property or the seizing that of others. Secure against the designs of men, secure against the malignity of the Gods, they have accomplished a thing of infinite difficulty; that to them nothing remains even to be wished."

A similar picture of the *skrithifinoi* (Sámi) appeared many times during the next thousand years. Tacitus' picture points out well that the Sámi's life was based on a hunting economy, not yet based on keeping reindeer. The basic pattern of the society was a community of Forest Sámi, whose annual migration included fishing, hunting and gathering according to the seasons. An especially important game animal was the wild reindeer, which was the basis for their trading activities.

Connections with the European trading system are seen in archaeological materials: locally made iron and ceramic items are missing from the finds. It was profitable for Sámi to specialize in hunting for furs, and therefore they did not need to bother with making iron. The importance of the interior of the land for reindeer hunting was emphasized by their nomadic way of life and for this heavy ceramic vessels were not suitable.

By the time of the Vikings, at the latest, the growth of hunting for furs led to the birth of winter villages for large communities. That may have been related to the beginnings of large systems of pits for killing reindeer; digging the pits and putting them to use requires extensive organization. The largest winter villages became places where merchants could easily visit, and later, tax collectors and officials.

Sámi were in the sphere of influence of many nationalities. Norwegian agricultural colonies had taken hold on the coast of the Arctic Ocean at least by around 200 AD, but stopped in the region of the Lofoten Islands and Romsa (Tromsa). Similarly, the Swedish advance northward remained for a long time south of the Ubmi River. Karelian merchants travelled by water routes from Lake Ladoga to the Gulf of Bothnia.

Around the northern shores of the Gulf of Bothnia lived the *Kvens*, and later the *Birkarls*, who controlled travel to Sápmi from their central settlements around the Gulf. According to current research, the name Birkarl does not refer to the place called *Pirkkala* in southern Finland, but rather it is a profession. The Birkarls were an association of merchants who had special rights to the Lapland trade, and later to taxation.

The emergence of the States' (Russia, Sweden, Denmark-Norway) interests in the North brought about changes in these interest groups and in Sámi relations. The States' borders in the North were still undefined at the end of the 1300s. They maintained spheres of influence with vague boundaries, the first being between Norway and Russia, agreed in 1251.

More precisely specified were the borders between Novgorod (Russia) and Sweden with the Nöteborg Peace Treaty of 1323. This treaty was an attempt to delineate the borders of Karelia and Savo in the East. In 1328 in the Telge Agreement,

Sweden strengthened its northern border at the Ubmi River, north of which agricultural settlement was forbidden. Both the Birkarls' and the Sámi's rights were protected against colonization.

However, the border set by the Nöteborg peace treaty immediately began to break down. Sweden began to "peacefully invade" the area north of the border. When settlers crossed the border they were promised freedom from military service and from taxation for a specified period. The invasion into the Novgorod sphere of interest, which reached into the North, caused 250 years of unrest and long lasting wars in which Sámi suffered. This may be the time known in the Sámi tradition as the čuđi Period. In folklore the čuđit were evil raiders who killed and destroyed everything.

The unrest was resolved by the Teusin Peace Treaty in 1595 in which the Swedish-Russian border was drawn, running from the Gulf of Finland through Guossan and Lake Anár to the Varanger Fjord on the Arctic Ocean coast. The Teusin peace treaty also deepened the separation of the eastern from the western Sámi culture. The eastern Sámi culture was marked by the Russian Orthodox religion and strong eastern traits. A lasting peace in the Sámi area was established and the spheres of influence were defined with the treaties of Knäred in 1613 and Stolbova in 1617.

Earlier research exaggerated the mongoloid traits in the Sámi population, they were by no means dominant. Mena Abrahamsen in 1884.

Forest Sámi and reindeer nomadism

The traditional Forest Sámi siida or Sámi village system is the prototype for Sámi society. It was a village unit that provided for community activities, and it was the area wherein the members of the society had usage rights. The siida owned a certain area that usually had well defined borders. The siida system was a permanent socio-economic and political institution and had been functional for centuries. Sámi were usually thought to have no permanent settlements or organizational structure before the colonists came into their area. That is why they were often referred to as "vagabond Lapps". According to current knowledge this picture is wrong. Sámi migrated for their livelihood, but only within their own carefully defined areas. The Swedish Crown recognized the siida boundaries and ownership rights until the 1700s.

The siida's communal lands and waters were divided into usage areas that were exclusive for kin groups or families. No one else had any business in these areas except those dealing with marriage negotiations or selling. Special "goahti (dwelling) assemblies" managed the area. This was the central management that decided and watched over the use areas, decided on usage rights, carried out administrative duties and other community business, such as presiding over marriages and accepting new members. All members of the siida had voting rights.

The organization of the Forest Sámi siida was based on annual migration. Kin groups and families stayed in their own areas from spring to fall, moving from one settlement site to another according to their fishing and hunting needs. At the height of winter the whole community gathered in the winter village, where merchants, tax collectors and ministers also knew to come. The Forest Sámi's multi-based livelihood depended on different

The administrative organization of the old siida structure lasted longest - until World War II - among the Skolt Sámi in Peäccam (Beahcán). Family members looked after common matters through the institution of the *sobbar*. Picture taken by Karl Nickul in Suo'nn'jel, 1934. Source: National Board of Antiquities and Historical Monuments, Helsinki.

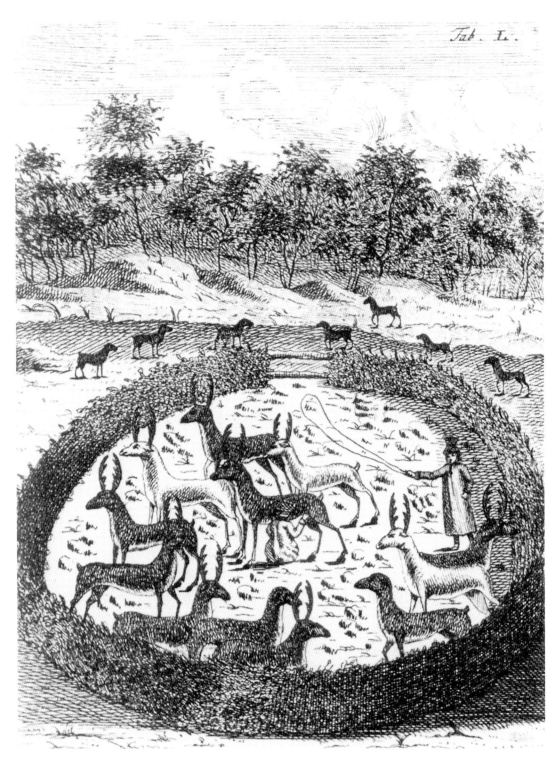

Small scale reindeer keeping, which included milking and some handling of reindeer, had its beginnings centuries earlier than regular nomadism in its complete form. Many later traits in reindeer herding, for example the use of the lasso, derived from methods applied in wild reindeer hunting. Drawing by Knud Leem 1767.

sources: freshwater fishing, hunting wild reindeer, snaring birds, sea fishing, picking berries and gathering; a sensitive usage of renewable natural resources.

The Forest Sámi siida system, which took on different forms depending on the natural conditions, underwent many kinds of changes from the 1500s onward. The outward reason was the States' influence and the spread of colonization. The internal reason was intense changes in livelihood that were related to the beginning of a new economic sector, nomadic reindeer herding, at the turn of the 1500s to the 1600s. Large-scale reindeer nomadism meant that reindeer herds dictated the lifestyle, its movements, land use and occupancy.

Reindeer keeping is divided into several developmental stages. Long before economically viable reindeer herding began, reindeer were tamed to use as draft and pack animals, and as lures to attract other reindeer. *Intensive reindeer keeping* had been practised, at least in the mountains of Sweden, probably since the 1400s. In addition to herding small groups of reindeer, reindeer milk was used for subsistence and reindeer calving was controlled in specific locations.

Extensive reindeer herding or full herding economy only developed later in a clearly defined era. According to records, the number of tamed reindeer grew in the early 1600s. For example, in the Luleju region their numbers exploded within just a few decades. The increase in tamed reindeer may be only statistical; perhaps the tax collectors only then began being interested in reindeer numbers. But it is obvious that larger changes are also linked to this question.

It is clear that full nomadism spread into different directions from the combined central areas of Luleju, Biton (Bihtán) and Ubmi. It is thought to have spread southwestward and northeastward from the Caledonian Ridge. It reached the present area of Finnish Lapland at the end of the 1600s, and only arrived in the Kola Peninsula in the 1800s.

It is also clear that the birth of *nomadic reindeer herding* is connected to the decrease of wild reindeer. In the mountains between the shores of the Arctic Ocean and Swedish Lapland, reindeer hunting had changed toward the end of the Middle Ages mostly due to over hunting because the

European market consumed endless quantities of furs. Pits and "corrals" for hunting constantly became bigger and on some mountains the corrals became giant sized. The entire herd would be driven into the corral and killed.

With the decrease of wild reindeer stock and the opening of pastures, reindeer keeping became a sensible way to continue the old livelihood. Hunting wild reindeer provided the most important basis for reindeer herding. The knowledge about wild reindeer, the terminology and techniques, tools and hunting systems were transferred to reindeer herding as special skills.

The change to reindeer herding meant a complete change in the way of life. It became full time work to enlarge the herds and to watch over each person's animals. The increase in numbers of reindeer led to a decrease in lichen vegetation in the traditional siida areas. It became necessary to travel far with the herd and to move the home along with it, taking the family too in order to keep it together. The herd had to be taken along on trips to the marketplaces, as well, because it could not be left unguarded.

In summer the migration route ended at the coast where there were fewer mosquitoes and more pleasant conditions for the reindeer. The forest pastures were left in peace for the summer. When autumn came they migrated back to the forest areas close to the tundra where the snow was softer than at the coast. The migration was suited to the rhythm of the seasons - at the cool coast in summer; in winter shielded from the winds in the forest - and made life easier in other ways.

Slaughtering was done at the coast in the fall, so the carcasses did not have to be carried long distances to market. It was also easier to migrate with the smaller herd. Besides the winter pasturing, they saved on the tax rolls in the winter village. In winter, possessions (and thus taxes) were fewer, but they increased in the fall for the markets.

These changes also caused a breakdown in the siida system. The Forest Sámi economic model based on distribution of surplus changed in the mountain areas to a system favouring private ownership and private enterprise. Nomadic reindeer herding was expansionist or rapidly spreading: lands were freely claimed for pastures, disturbing the situation of other Sámi groups.

Large scale reindeer herding changed the livelihood of the Forest Sámi completely: their diverse economy was now replaced by reindeer herding as the main activity. Picture of Oula Piera by E. N. Manninen, Deatnu, 1930s. Source: Eila Lahti's archive.

A "reindeer village" was not founded on the traditional siida practice of exclusive kin group communities; it could be formed of independent units and families. Under the influence of nomadic reindeer herding, the structure of the siida also changed. Small square areas used by the Forest Sámi became long shaped siidas or "reindeer villages". The summer residences could be hundreds of kilometies from the winter settlements.

Reindeer nomadism had many consequences. The expansionist nature caused competition for pastures among siidas as well as among other Sámi groups, for instance, the Sea Sámi. The emphasis on private ownership led to the emergence of differences in wealth and even to capitalism, which had the trait of following the modern "principle of constant growth and the expectation of unlimited growth" (expressed in modern terminology).

On the other hand, it is said that the Reindeer Sámi had the most secure social system of all the Sámi and of the colonizing settlers. Their food supply exceeded their own needs, and poorer members were provided with reindeer meat to feed themselves. Nomadism encouraged specialization because herders did not make all of their equipment: the *gieres* (reindeer sled), for instance, was made by Sámi craftsmen or by Finns.

Regardless of the fact that full reindeer herding is an historically "young" phenomenon in Sámi culture and that the Forest Sámi way of life came to be preserved as the basic mode of Sámi society, reindeer nomadism came to be, in the following centuries, the central characteristic and dominant livelihood of the Sámi people. As a widespread form it nevertheless did not persist longer than two hundred years.

A NATURAL PEOPLE´S MENTAL LANDSCAPE

The traditions and history of Sámi religious culture are difficult to trace. The religious culture underwent violent changes in connection with Christian missionizing in the 1600s and 1700s. Most of the symbolism of the noaidi drums was lost. It is difficult to reconstruct completely the old world-view from sources written by outsiders. Much of the relationship of the oral tradition and the yoik tradition to the shamanistic world-view going back hundreds of years is hidden in shadow.

The intent of Christian priests seems to have been the complete destruction of the old world-view, not just the shamanic practices. Besides the traditions firmly linked to shamanism, the church judged many other unfamiliar customs to be heathen, such as the secular yoik tradition.

Information on the speed and success of the conversion process is contradictory. Clergymen reported that Christianization proceeded well and smoothly; for such success they would have been rewarded by being transferred to somewhere warmer and "closer to civilization". The 1670s is held to be the decade when Torneå Lapland and Kemi Lapland were converted to Christianity. However, many inspection visits by the Church at the end of the 1600s indicate that, for instance, in Torneå Lapland the report of Christianization was just empty words.

Recent Sámi research has criticized the picture of the missionizing work as too simplistic. The tendency of the Lapland missionaries to regard Sámi mythology as nothing more than a collection of undeveloped beliefs

was also reflected in the views of scholars. A typical example was in T. I. Itkonen's book *Suomen lappalaiset vuoteen 1945* (Finland's Lapps to the year 1945) where he carefully differentiated "folklore" and "mythology" and, later, "belief in magic".

Recent research regards the old shamanism as a part of the whole world-view, rather than a religion or superstition. The varied oral tradition and yoiks are fragmentary remains of that world-view. Because conversion was a matter of replacing the complete world-view, it probably, despite force, was nowhere near complete in a few decades.

Old customs were preserved for a long time at least in some form. For example in Anár (Aanaar), offerings which would earlier have been taken to the sieidis were instead, for many decades, brought to the church at Peälbájävri. Christian views and imagery still were filtered through the old religion. Elements of the old religion continued to survive "in mothballs" even until the 1800s.

The culture of making sacrificial offerings, worshipping at shrines and using drums became secret; the "gods" above ground moved underground, becoming "earth spirits". More decisive was the crumbling of the old foundations of the society that came in the 1800s. With that, previous customs became superstitions or ideas that were preserved in all the other (Christian) deceptions.

A people´s world-view

The world-view of the Sámi hunting society and, later, the

nomadic society reflected their adaptation to the northern environment and the way of living there. The mythology of that society closely bound to nature depicts ideas linked to wild reindeer, bears and other animals. The cosmos of this people, who practised a lifestyle of migration, followed cycles symbolizing the cycle of the year and cycle of life.

In the old culture, human relationships with the two realms of reality, the physical world ("this side") and the spiritual world ("the other side"), were bridged by the activities of special men and women - *noaidi*. Just as the world was divided into the seen and the unseen, the tangible and the intangible, so human beings were composed of two parts: the body soul and the free soul.

In a non-active state - in dream, trance or coma - a free soul may leave the body and take on another form outside of the person. The noaidi had the skill to reach this state at will. It is described in different ways. The *noaidi* in a trance leaves the body and moves as a spirit or breath of wind. They have the ability to change into a wild reindeer or hide under the reindeer's neck or hoof; they can fly over the treetops or travel under the ground; they may swim in the shape of a fish; and the Sea Sámi recount that they may even move mountains.

The traditional shamanism was an integral and essential part of the hunting culture. Shamanic activities were related to crisis situations in a village or family; the *noaidi* attempted to find a remedy. The greatest crises for this people dependent on nature were illnesses and problems concerning obtaining a livelihood. Illness is a disturbance of the balance between the two souls and between the two realms of reality. The *noaidi*, in spirit form, leaves and goes to "the other side" to restore harmony. Innumerable tales relating to obtaining a livelihood and epic poems tell that a "trance noaidi" was able to control the movements of a whole reindeer herd.

Apparently it is the precise knowledge of nature that was the basis of "controlling the weather and reindeer herds", which ancient sources tell us the Sámi were capable of doing. According to one writer, "the 'Finnlapp' is able to raise any kind of wind he wishes". It probably was a matter of making predictions by using signs in nature that seers were masters at recognizing through the traditional knowledge of many thousands of years. When seen from outside, these predictions were wrongly interpreted as commanding natural phenomena.

This belief led hopeful travellers from Central Europe to come to buy wind from Sámi. One of them boasted of getting one for the ridiculously low price of ten crowns and a pound of tobacco.

Transforming traditions

Under the stern Christianization, the great noaidi - those who had the power of ecstasy - appear to have disappeared by the 1800s. The "second-rate quacks" were the only remnants. Some people posed as noaidi for tourists, making predictions using alcohol, which is more a reflection of the far-reaching advance of alcoholism rather than the shamanistic tradition. The great noaidi appear to have remained longest in Kola Lapland; the Russian Orthodox church did not persecute noaidi so severely.

By the 1800s shamanism had been

The noaidi's most important instrument was the noaidi drum. It was a tool to enter the ecstatic state as well as a "map" the noaidi used for orientation in the other realm. Drawing by Knud Leem in 1767.

replaced by a network of healers and seers who were Christian. In the place of trips to "the other side" and helpful guiding spirits, the seers relied on charms and concentrated on "this side" activities. The seers lost or gave up their actual connection with the other realm, along with direct "knowledge of its terrain".

"The other side" became the enemy of the Christian seers, whose lives related to the new agricultural economy; in the same way nature became an enemy against which they struggled as peasant farmers. The shamanistic fundamental deep knowledge of nature was preserved with the seers for a long time. As an example, a well-known seer from the upper reaches of the Duortnus

River, Hukka-Salkko, healed "aches and pains" and injuries, stopped bleeding, abolished nightmares, cured epileptics, put evil spells on thieves, commanded fire and water, and even bullets so that they had no effect on him.

The image of noaidi-ism changed because of Christian belief. During the era of the witch hunts the word noaidi clearly took on a negative meaning. All people who practised the old religion were held to be people who had given themselves to immorality or the Devil - they were believed to have sold their own souls, their relatives' and even their children's souls. This belief persisted even into the 1900s.

The encroachment of the nation-states

At the same time as the birth of reindeer nomadism, there were other upheavals caused by outside influences. From the 1500s onward, the governments of the Nordic countries attempted to convert their northern spheres of influence into fixed parts of their nations. There were three main ways in which this happened: Christian missionizing, social control and colonization.

Missionizing at the coast of the Arctic Ocean and around the Gulf of Bothnia had begun with the building of churches in the 1100s; in Russian Lapland in the 1400s. Progress had been slow into the 1500s, when the Norwegian Sea Sámi were converted to the Christian faith, "although they don't know what to do with that information", as one of the state representatives reported.

In Sweden, missionizing intensified at the turn of the 1600s when Karl IX actively began to organize it. The intensification of missionizing was closely linked to political interests. The sovereignty over the northern regions was unclear; Sweden from the beginning saw missionizing as a mark of her claim to rights of possession and taxation.

Karl IX increased the activities of ministers in all parts of Lapland and actively began to build churches. The power relations in the North were clarified in the first decade of the 1600s, though not exactly as Sweden had wished. In the Teusin Peace Treaty (1595), Sweden expanded her kingdom at Russia's expense, but in 1613 in the Knäred Peace Treaty she lost the possibility of reaching the coast of the Arctic Ocean. Norway got possession of the coastal zone, and Sweden handed over the taxation rights to the Arctic Ocean coast that she had but recently gained from Russia. The Stolbova Peace Treaty of 1617 defined the border between Sweden-Finland and Russia.

Although churches were built in Kemi Lapland and Torneå Lapland, there were plenty of problems for their missionizing. Torneå Lapland was a large, extensive region, reaching as far north as Ohcejohka. Kemi Lapland included the old Russian area, in which the taxation rights and religious situation were still unsettled. For a long time the clergymen still lived outside of Lapland in towns on the coasts of the Gulf of Bothnia and rarely visited the siidas in Lapland. When they did, it seems they did as much trading as actual missionizing. In Kemi Lapland, ministers resided permanently in their parishes from around 1650 onward.

The language problem hampered the teaching of Christian beliefs. Sámi was certainly used in missionizing. Already in 1619 the first book in a Sámi language, an alphabet book, was published by Nicolaus Andrae, the minister of the Ubmi parish. For the next century an abundance of religious literature appeared in Sámi languages.

When Johannes Tornaeus came to Torneå Lapland in 1640, he immediately began training local Sámi speaking assistants. There are known to have been ten Sámi ministers in Sweden in the 1600s. The first Sámi minister in Kemi Lapland was Olaus Sirma, who was educated in Uppsala and was active in Eanodat from 1676 until his death in 1719.

In addition to religious ministration, the States attempted to bring the siidas in Lapland into their secular administrative spheres. State organized assemblies held during market times began to replace the traditional goahti assemblies. Replacing the siida Elder as the highest authority came representatives of the kings: bailiffs, who functioned as judges of the assembly and as tax collectors, and who had other administrative responsibilities, as well.

It had been thought that by 1600 the Crown itself owned the lands and waters of the Lapland siidas. However, recent research has shown that that idea was wrong. Kaisa Korpijaakko's research on the legal history of Swedish-Finnish Lapland revealed that Sámi property rights were comparable to the Nordic laws of ownership and they endured without conflict and were recognized by the authorities of the Crown until at least 1750.

The States' hold on Lapland in the 1600s was not as self-evident as research has traditionally understood it to be. Further, it has been shown that in both religious and secular realms new patterns and old traditions continued side by side for a long time. Research is only just beginning to look at their mutual influence. The balance changed radically during the 1700s, leading to the collapse of the siida system.

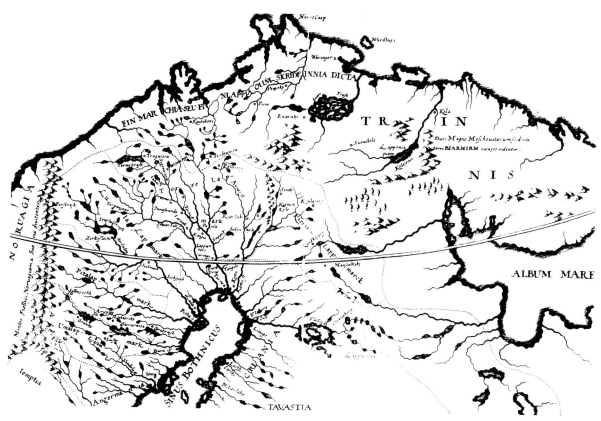

Information about the northern areas of Scandinavia became more widespread in the 1500s. The first complete representation of Sámi was Joannis Schefferus' *Lapponia* (1673). It painted a very true picture of Lapland.

Agricultural colonizers and the Sámi

Colonization had an even more devastating impact on Sámi culture from the 1600s to the 1800s. Still in the 1500s, on the Norwegian and Swedish side, colonization actually stopped at the "borders of Lapland", both because of the natural and political conditions. Norwegian colonization reached as far as just south of Romsa (Tromsa); cultivation was not feasible farther north. On the Swedish side, until the 1500s, the clear policy of the Crown was to respect the rights of the influential Birkarls in the region of the Gulf of Bothnia. In the Finnish area, for hundreds of years, the Sámi population came increasingly under the feet of Finnish colonizers.

In Sweden, the Lapland Border, separating cultivation and reindeer herding areas, was strengthened against colonists; it clearly partitioned the new colonial settlement areas from lands belonging to Sámi. In the time of King Gustav Wasa in 1543, Sámi rights to hunt on both sides of this border were expanded, but peasants and colonists were strictly forbidden from penetrating across the border. Karl IX further enforced the Lapland Border, with certain exceptions, in the beginning of the 1600s.

Until the end of the 1600s, it was not possible to colonize the lands of Sámi siidas. According to the laws of Sweden, the land belonged to the members of the siidas. Many court proceedings from the end of the 1600s prove that the Lapland Border was indeed maintained in practice. Court judgements consistently recognized that the members of the Sámi siidas were the landowners, and the judgements were made in favour of the Sámi.

The situation changed due to the colonization decrees, called placards, issued by the Swedish

31

Crown in 1673 and 1695. The premise of the decrees was that the livelihoods of the Sámi and of the colonists could exist side by side without detriment to either one. For the Reindeer Sámi in Torneå Lapland these placards did not cause problems. On the other hand, this concept of living side by side produced disastrous consequences for the Forest Sámi of Kemi Lapland.

In just the opposite from what was intended, colonists exploded into Kemi Lapland. The rush to colonize, along with the destruction of Sámi livelihood through the colonists' slash and burn cultivation method, pushed into the Guossan (Kuusamo) and Giiggajávri (Kitkajärvi) area where the situation became fateful. Within two decades the old Sámi siidas of Giiggajávri and Másealgi (Maaselkä) were taken over by farmers raising cattle and practising agriculture. The placards thus violated their original intents.

The effects of the colonization placards on Kemi Lapland should not be exaggerated, though. Farther north the rush was quite small. There the official position still prevailed that the Sámi siidas owned the area. Court documents clearly show that, long into the 1700s, rulings consistently went against the colonists. In general, conflicts over fishing places and hunting also were decided in favour of the Sámi.

Colonists received access to the area only with permission of a Sámi siida. They could marry a Sámi or buy or rent land from them. However, some colonists did manage, by lengthy creeping tactics, to force their way into lands belonging to the Sámi siidas. This became common in the 1700s.

In the 1700s the situation changed. The rights of the Sámi siidas were no longer honoured - the old Lapland Border between Lapland and the South was gradually forgotten.

The case of Finnish colonization of the Soadegilli region at the end of the 1600s was marked by Sámi themselves even becoming colonists. There are many examples of how Sámi used the situation to their advantage by becoming colonists on their own taxation lands.

At first the change from Sámi to Finnish settlement was only through documentation in which new Sámi "colonists" were considered to be "Finns" because of the change in livelihood. A Sámi, who had formerly been called a "Lapp" because he engaged in a nature-based livelihood, was now listed as a "Finn" because of his new profession based on agricultural colonization. The Sami's newly founded colonial farm was registered, and the building obligation was determined and recorded in the registry. His dwelling place was given a Finnish name, which then became his descendants' surname.

The year in which the last Sámi resident of a region founded his farm is the point when "Lapps" are considered to have been "expelled", or actually exterminated, from that area. For more southerly areas those years are Pudasjärvi and Giepma 1683, Taivalkoski 1668, Savukoski 1700, Kuolajärvi 1740, and Guossan 1738.

The process was clearly linked to cultural change. When Sámi became colonists and joined the Finnish village network, they adapted their way of life to the Finnish style and adopted the Finnish language. Being Sámi came to be shameful. Sámi even started speaking Finnish with their children in the hope that they would be more successful in the new environment. By the next generation, or sooner, the Finnish name of the farm became their official family name.

The old property rights of the members of Sámi siidas, which had still been secure in the early 1700s, became obscured by the 1800s. The precise time when the authorities started to sidestep the law is still unclear. According to some, the order given to the bailiffs in 1745 and the Lapland rules of 1749 brought about this change in the practices of the local authorities.

On the Finnish side, a turning point was the advent of Finland gaining autonomous status after being ceded to Russia by Sweden in 1809. The authorities as well as the old administrative practices of the Swedish realm changed under Russian rule. Revocation and abrogation of Sámi rights was not based on statutory laws, but rather on practices that took shape gradually.

Kongl. Maj:ts
PLACAT,
Angående Lappmarckernes bebyggiande.

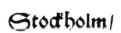

Stockholm/

Tryckt hoos Nicolaum Wankijff/ Kongl. Booktr.

27 Septemb 1673

C

The Swedish kings attempted to protect the Sámi settlements from the pressure of colonization. Nevertheless, decrees, called placards, for colonization were posted in 1673 and 1695 sealing the fate of the Sámi *siidas*.

SÁMI WRITTEN CULTURE

In the 1700s a remarkable change occurred in the Sámi relationship to written culture. The church, in its attempt to educate the Sámi and thereby promote their acceptance of Christianity, established a network of catechists, a school system suited to conditions in Lapland. It proved to be such a good innovation that it was maintained in the Sámi area as the main educational model for nearly 200 years. The catechists were travelling teachers, who often were local people and spoke Sámi.

The idea of having Sámi as teachers originated as early as the 1600s. Swedish and Finnish speaking ministers had a hard time learning Sámi and, so, often sought to teach by force. Because of the difficulties in teaching, the important role of the mother tongue in facilitating learning probably was understood from the beginning. It is known that Sámi speaking boys were sent to study in Uppsala in 1606, but with no success.

In 1616, in Biton (Bihtán), Sámi boys were trained to be ministers, and the first real school in Lapland was founded in Likšu in 1632. The founder of the school in Biton (Bihtán), Nicolaus Andrae, published the first books in a Sámi language in 1619: a missal and an alphabet book. Otherwise the use of Sámi language in teaching proceeded badly. On the Norwegian side, a seminary established in Trondheim in the beginning of the 1700s taught teachers and ministers who were to go to the Sámi.

In Swedish Lapland teaching was strengthened when, in 1723, a royal decree caused the establishment of schools, which were to be connected to the main churches. Sámi were to be taught in their own language, so the ministers needed to learn Sámi as well. Nevertheless, the schools did not get pupils; the migratory lifestyle was not suited to a stationary school. A pedagogical school founded in Ohcejohka to train Sámi speaking teachers functioned for only seven years. On the Norwegian side, Sámi language was replaced by Danish in 1773.

The only model that functioned was the catechists' teaching. In Ohcejohka it began in 1751; catechists came to Anár (Aanaar) and Eanodat thirty years later. The goal of training catechists was to promote literacy and in that way spread the message of Christianity. The aim was to achieve through teaching the same level in Lapland as in the rest of the realm, thereby bringing "basic civilization" to this peripheral population.

The catechists travelled from one village, house or goahti to the next and taught the nearby children for a week or two at a time. The parents provided them with food and clothing. The State paid them a salary. It was normal for catechists to participate in the work of the household, act as a nurse and preside over religious events, holding prayer meetings and sermons.

In the beginning, nearly all catechists were Sámi, a fact that meant they were very influential locally. Using the Sámi language in teaching opened the way to developing it as a written language. Until the end of the 1800s almost all literature in Sámi was religious. The first viable Sámi language newspaper *Nuorttanaste* was religious. Sámi religious circles maintained high regard for Sámi as a written and semi-official language, even after it was shamed into obscurity.

In official Church circles the relationship to Sámi language varied. There was always opposition to teaching in Sámi. It was tried to substitute Sámi with Finnish, the other minority language in the Swedish kingdom. As early as the 1700s, the ministers in Guossan gave corporal punishment to Sámi who did not speak Finnish properly. This was, however, forbidden by the Church authorities. In 1751 the governing body of the Church in Lapland decided to discontinue Sámi as the obligatory teaching language. They approved the use of Finnish in its place, "because it is believed that the more the Sámi language declines, the more the people will progress toward knowledge and manners". A Finnish minister in Giepma and provincial dean at the end of the 1700s, labelled Sámi the "devil's language". In Norway the handling of the language dispute was not much different. A Norwegian clergyman exclaimed that even God cannot understand Sámi.

The position of the Sámi language on the Norwegian side constantly declined throughout the 1800s with the Norwegianization policy; although Nils Vibe Stockfleth, for one, did valuable work to further Sámi as a written language. In Sweden and in autonomous Finland under Russia, despite opposition, Sámi language teaching made clear progress in the 1800s. The most important advocates were Jacob Fellman and Lars Levi Laestadius.

köölöh
Joo päätteh kärven küdtjärah;
Häälak, hvomahah, baaron baakasah;
Neitavuotas vuurtás tjuolmau luoitaa.
Tait negga pärjasit nuusi,
160 Jahnam jaskesahtaa,
Paaroit paishesathaa;
Jeuke Jehtarah naatseh.
Tjäunskaliin tjuudáidás airoit,
Pevasah påhtjasiin Tjälmüst
165 Kälme, hastem, nehtem, aiks,
Jappee uudda, märee tuöttaa —
Väsje makoeties moittaa;
Tjälmeh tjeskeh, vaimo vuoje täüsaa
Hääja juovagit haaliddaa.

Until the 1800s Sámi literature was religious, and the first literary texts were written by ministers or preachers. The Suorssá minister Anders Fjellner (1795-1876) compiled the epic "Sons of the Sun" based on poems he collected and which perhaps also incorporated his own compositions.

Other than religious texts, the only published works written in Sámi before the 1800s were some individual poems. The best known are two poems by Olaus Sirma published in the 1600s, which were included in Joannis Schefferus' book *Lapponia* (1673). They were admired by poets such as J. G. von Herder and H. W. Longfellow, and by the Finnish poets J. L. Runeberg and F. M. Franzén.

The first works in prose by Sámi portraying their own background were written in the 1800s. Two pioneers of Sámi literature were Lars Haetta and Anders Baer; both were Laestadian zealots living in Guovdageaidnu, and both landed in prison for their part in the Guovdageaidnu Uprising in 1852. While in prison they wrote their autobiographical accounts of the old Sámi way of life and beliefs. Their chronicles were not published during their lifetime, but only saw the light of day in 1958 with the publication of the complete original texts - *Mui'talusat* (Memoirs).

In the mid 1800s, the Sámi minister Anders Fjellner began working on a Sámi national epic poem in the style of the Finnish *Kalevala*. Elias Lönnrot, between 1838 and 1849, had compiled the Finnish national epic poem *Kalevala*, which was all important in the creation of the Finnish national identity. Fjellner understood the symbolic value of a national epic.

From collected, or even personally invented, "folk poems" he prepared an anthology entitled *Beaivve bártnit* (Sons of the Sun). However, only parts of it were published. Because the complete epic was never found among Fjellner's papers, we do not even know if it ever existed.

The greatest reason Fjellner did not carry the project to completion seems to have been that the situation in Sápmi, unlike in Finland, was not yet ripe for the awakening of an ethnic consciousness. Local communities endured as distinct enclaves for a long time so that there could be no basis for national solidarity among Sámi, not even in intellectual circles.

From special rights to the border closings

In the century from 1751 to 1852 the Sámi position in relation to the States changed drastically. The year 1751 is a central one in Sámi history. In that year the Strömstad Border Treaty was concluded between Sweden and Norway. Formally the issue concerned taxation of Sámi practising reindeer nomadism - they would no longer be taxed by both countries but would only pay taxes to one country even though they made their livelihood in both.

The treaty defined the Norwegian-Swedish border to run from the northern part of Gilbbesjávri to Golmmešoaivi along the line which later was to become the northern border between Finland and Norway. Guovdageaidnu and Ávjovárri and the western part of Tanaby became part of Norway. The eastern part of Tanaby and Anár (Aanaar) were joined to Ohcejohka which became part of Kemi Lapland. As far as the Sámi were concerned, the most important part of the treaty was the appendix, the "Lapp Codicil", which officially spelled out the special rights of Sámi.

The guiding principle in the treaty was "the conservation of the Lappish nation" (in Norwegian, "den lappiske nationens konservation"), the preservation of the Sámi people. The most important article concerned the Sámi's right to move freely across the borders. It guaranteed the rights of Sámi to move in their traditional way, disregarding the borders, from the inland to the ocean coast, and confirmed their rights to hunt, move reindeer herds and even to sell. It strengthened the rights of Sámi from the Swedish side, for instance from Lake Anár (Aanaarjávri), to fish freely on the Norwegian coast.

The second crucial item concerned Sámi status during wartime. The text states that wars must not cause any changes whatsoever in the situation of the Sámi; thus, "they are always to be regarded and treated as their own subjects, no matter on which side of the border they are". The article was interpreted to mean that Sámi could not be conscripted, officially confirming the traditional Sámi right to be freed from military service.

A drawback in the agreement was that, unlike the Teusin Peace Treaty, in which the border followed the siida boundaries, the Strömstad Treaty did not; it split the Deatnu in two, for example. No new rights were granted to the Sámi. They now had to choose a citizenship and by that their land ownership was affected.

Nevertheless, the appendix in the Strömstad Treaty is regarded as so important that it has been called the "Sámi Magna Carta". Karl Nickul was of the opinion that the States had clear knowledge that they were dividing the Sámi lands with this treaty, but that it must not have a negative effect on their livelihoods.

The situation of the Sámi changed decisively in the 1800s when Sápmi, the Sámi homeland, was split into four parts by the national borders. In 1809 Finland came into the Russian Empire as a Grand Duchy with its own laws. That meant the border between Sweden and Finland became more well-defined and the Sámi siidas were attached to one or the other of these states. In 1826 the Njauddâm (Njávdán) area that had remained jointly taxed by Russia and Norway was made a part of Norway.

These agreements, negating the Strömstad Treaty, prohibited crossing the borders freely. Reindeer nomads were prohibited from crossing the border; likewise residents of the Finnish side were denied the right to fish in the Várjavuotna. These restrictions were not yet enforced. Norway made it more difficult for foreigners to fish at the coast of the Arctic Ocean, and Russia complained about the nomads spending time on the Finnish side.

These differences of opinion led to the closure of the Norwegian-Finnish border by the Russian Tsar in 1852. The Strömstad Treaty was thus no longer valid. This measure was good luck for reindeer herding in Finnish Lapland, but the border closing caused upheaval for Sámi culture. Along with the closing of the Finnish-Swedish border in 1889 it spelled the destruction of reindeer nomadism.

The border closures cut off traditional, long migration routes which had shaped reindeer Sámi society for hundreds of years. Their plight was especially visible in the tundra area of Norway. When the border prevented them from crossing into Eanodat (Finland) and into Sweden, the pressure was directed towards the Guovdageaidnu winter pastures where reindeer were already abundant.

The situation resulted in mass migrations of Reindeer Sámi. They were obliged to choose the state in which they would take up residency. The Reindeer Sámi of Guovdageaidnu moved to Eanodat and Soabbat on the Finnish side and to the Swedish side, mostly to Gáresávvon. Between 1853 and 1882 as many as three hundred Sámi moved to Gáresávvon, from where, as Swedish subjects, they were allowed to pasture their animals on the Finnish side until they were prevented by the closing of that border as well.

The change in settlement of Soabbat in Soadegilli was a consequence of the border closure. The original Forest Sámi population had been assimilated as Finns at the end of the 1700s and a reindeer pestilence had destroyed the local reindeer keeping. Now a new Sámi group, the Reindeer Sámi, moved into the area from the west. Within several decades, from 1870 to the beginning of the 1900s, among others came the families *Nikodemus, Peltovuoma, Ponku, Turi, Hirvasvuopio* and *Länsman*.

Reindeer Sámi also came into Anár (Aanaar) from the North. When access to the Arctic Ocean coast was cut off, the pressure overflowed into western Anár (Aanaar) to the Gihttel border, where they had been coming to pasture for a long time. Families that moved into western Anár (Aanaar) were *Jomppanen, Kitti, Länsman* and *Aikio*. New residents of northeastern Anár (Aanaar) were the *Sauva, Boine, Panne, Holmberg* and *Högman* families. New names along the shores of the Avvil (Avveel) River in southern Anár (Aanaar) were *West* and *Aikio*.

The significance of the Sámi's adaptation in this crisis must be emphasized. Sudden observance of the rules preventing migration would have destroyed the entire reindeer economy of that time. Nevertheless, the Sámi were able to preserve the pattern of their traditional life for some time longer. As time went by they either had to give up migrating or try to conceal it somehow.

For a long time the situation was confused. Sámi moved back and forth from one state to another: many moved only on paper. Some lost their reindeer, others got the beginnings of a herd from stray reindeer. Whole reindeer households were lost or newly established. The consequences of the border closures were harsh. The traditional annual migrations were drastically shortened. For example, the siidas in the Finnish and Swedish areas were faced with adjusting their lives to an inland existence, since they were not allowed to go to the Arctic Ocean coast - with a few exceptions.

Likewise in Norway the Reindeer Sámi had to be satisfied in their more northern winter areas; the sheltered forests close to the tundra on the Finnish side were forbidden to their reindeer. The large reindeer herds began to dwindle. The overcrowding and small numbers of reindeer led to herding becoming a secondary livelihood on the model of the Forest Sámi. At the same time remaining longer in one area led to a more permanent mode of dwelling.

The border closure of 1852 also caused the beginning of the end of fishing at the Arctic Ocean coast for Sámi from the Finnish side. Norway already had restricted fishing rights in 1871. Fishing restrictions were also set on the most important Sámi waterways. The first official fishing regulations for the Deatnu in 1872-1873 brought an end to the fish weirs stretching clear across the river that were used jointly from the Norwegian and Finnish sides.

THE SÁMI AND THE LAESTADIAN FAITH

The Laestadian faith has from its beginning been an important part of Sámi culture. It influences - positively and negatively - many Sámi even today. The movement's first centre was Gáresávvon; later the movement formed strong centres around Kárášjohka and the Deatnu River valley.

The Laestadian faith is usually thought to be the result of the activities of one man, Lars Levi Laestadius, who may have been somewhat influenced by the revivalist movement in the Nordic countries. Since about 1860 it has been known as a characteristic movement among Finns, which split into many different directions.

Only in recent research has light been shed on the historical Sámi beginnings of the movement. In his doctoral thesis, Nilla Outakoski emphasized that Laestadius' background had strong connections to the Sámi area. Laestadius was the third generation of a family of Lutheran ministers in Lapland and grew up on the edges of three different Sámi cultures; he was born in Ume Lapland, his mother was a Sámi from Bihtán and as a child he lived in Lule Lapland.

In childhood Laestadius already knew two or three Sámi languages. Later he learned a fourth, North Sámi, the main language of the Reindeer Sámi. Through his own work he developed a blended language, "Tent Sámi", which he used in his preaching. Laestadius created a written language that was only used by one person - Laestadius himself!

Laestadius' Sámi cultural background can be seen mainly in his incorporation of certain supernatural beings from Sámi mythology. Before his spiritual conversion he did research on Sámi mythology in his unpublished book *Fragmenter i lappisk mythologi* (Fragments in Lappish Mythology). After his conversion he used lore from his research to combat the old beliefs, and to try to reach Sámi with his preaching by entering into their thought process.

Outakoski explains that the reason the Laestadian movement spread "like wildfire" was because of the existence of the *čuorvvut* movement, originated in the 1700s in Guovdageaidnu, which had become central among Reindeer Sámi. The *čuorvvut* movement was similar to the later Laestadian movement; it had the characteristics of severe fundamentalist preaching and states of ecstasy. Its name "shouters" or "callers" came from travelling preachers, who loudly preached hellfire and damnation and admonished people to repent.

Having been brought up in the Sámi religious tradition, Laestadius received his revelation through his acquaintance with a Sámi religious woman - later called "Maria of Lapland". After Laestadius had his revelation and began to preach with conviction and passion, the *čuorvvut* recognized him as one of their own kind. His reputation spread, since followers of the *čuorvvut* movement were found from the distant Arctic Ocean coast to Pajala at the Torneå River.

The first followers of Laestadianism were Mountain Sámi. There were plenty of Sámi preachers who travelled widely over large areas on their migration routes. Even so, the movement never spread into some areas, for instance Luleå Lapland. In the beginning phase of Laestadianism, Laestadius trained these preachers himself. Two of his pupils, Lars Haetta and Anders Baer, took part in the Guovdageaidnu Uprising (see below).

Sin and moral decline

In addition to being based on the old beliefs, another reason for the spread of Laestadian awakening was the state of society and morals in the Sámi area. The background for this revival movement was clearly presented in the "Memoirs" of Lars Haetta and Anders Baer, which were first published much later (*Mui'talusat*, 1958).

Haetta and Baer were hardline Laestadians, whose writings are filled with intensely fundamental religious texts and ecstasy. As an historical document the book describes everyday life of the Reindeer Sámi's migratory life in the beginning of the 1800s before the time of Laestadius. It contains a valuable contemporary view of those times, giving views on many things that were later disputed, above all views regarding the old Sámi religious beliefs and Laestadianism.

Haetta is very reminiscent of his mentor Laestadius in his strict style and the examples in his repentance sermons. He writes at length about the moral decline of Sámi society and their many sins which Laestadius attacked in the end. Haetta very clearly, in simple language, brings to light bare facts of the alarming extent of the rise of

Laestadians gathering in front of their meeting house in the Deatnu region in the 1930s. Source: National Board of Antiquities and Historical Monuments, Helsinki.

alcoholism. As an authority on the second sin of reindeer theft, Haetta wrote a study of rare quality.

Viewed as equally rare is his concise "presentation" on the third sin, the old Sámi religion, about which only Johan Turi gave an equally competent description from his own time. Haetta's attitude toward noaidi-ism is the genuine scepticism of a fundamentalist (he uses the word "supposedly" 16 times in his short two paged description), but his knowledge of its use is, from a scientific standpoint, extremely valuable.

Baer tells, in his description, of his "year of decision" through his own experiences and his own life. Describing a young man struggling to free himself from his controlling and boozing father, he depicts it through a Reindeer Sámi family's everyday life. His images are bleak, "My father was a heavy drinker.

Drinking until he was drunk, father sometimes would try to teach me the Lord's Prayer, but he couldn't recite it himself; he had forgotten everything after his time in school."

In a literary style, Baer describes growing up in an unstable family, a meaningless life of drink, rumours and religious revelation making "the people of Gáresávvon lose their reason".

Baer's line of fire is very clearly aimed at official church beliefs and ministers, characterized by him in many pointed images. He describes at great length ministers for whom he was a driver; drinking during the whole trip, the clergyman no longer was able to speak clearly, finally could not even feed himself, "and he could not be distinguished from a simple drunken Sámi."

A special event in the church was related to minister Stockfleth, a well-known minister in Lapland. In

Baer's description, he boxed the pupils' ears with the New Testament and most angrily those of a boy named Ásllat Haetta. That boy later became the leader of the 1852 uprising in Guovdageaidnu in which Stockfleth's follower was beaten.

In Laestadius' strict world-view, many Sámi found a solution to the difficulties brought by the insecure times. For some, like Lars Haetta and Anders Baer, their fate led to another extreme, religious fanaticism. They were imprisoned for their part in the Guovdageaidnu Uprising. Despite their dismal fate, in prison Lars Haetta and Anders Baer were in their own way "privileged". They became pioneers of Sámi literature, writing their memoirs and teaching others of their kind to read and write.

GUOVDAGEAIDNU´S FANATICS –
RELIGIOUS FERVOUR OR FOLK UPRISING?

Known in history as Europe's most peaceful people, the Sámi have had only one violent incident, but it was most ferocious. On Monday, November 8, 1852 in Guovda-geaidnu, Norway, a group of Sámi religious fanatics killed a merchant and the policeman and beat the local preacher nearly to death. The reason for the killings is thought to have been caused by wrongly directed Laestadian zealousness, but Sámi researchers, in particular, have emphasized that the event also had a societal nature.

In 1979-80, at the height of the Álta Conflict, some hardline Sámi brought forward the Guovdageaidnu event as the first milestone of the Sámi struggle as a nation. Nevertheless, the Guovdageaidnu Uprising has never received general approval among Sámi, but rather the opposite.

The words to the well-known old yoik, "Guovdageaidnu bloody knife", is a reminder among the older generation of this horror, which they were told about in their childhood. The Sámi writers Pedar Jalvi and Johan Turi also wrote about it in negative tones.

The event is also in the memory of younger people. For the Nordic Theatre course organized in Anár (Aanaar) at the end of the 1980s, there were plans to produce a drama about the events in Guovdageaidnu. However, the participants from the Norwegian side, mainly Guovdageaidnu residents, rejected the project. Among them were descendants of people imprisoned for the uprising; to them the wounds were still too painful.

A revival movement?

The starting point of the uprising and the official instigator was Lars Levi Laestadius' revivalist acti-vities, which at the beginning had support mainly among Reindeer Sámi. The strength of Laes-tadianism was based above all on "cleansing", with which it rid Sámi society of alcohol and other vices introduced by neighbouring peop-les from south of Sápmi.

These same vices also had an influence on the society in the part of Sápmi in northern Norway. Norwegian colonization pressures in Sápmi, after a century long pause, had again begun to grow in the 1800s, and now received state support. In this invasion of the best fishing places and netting grounds, the Norwegians very often were protected by new laws and local courts.

Sámi were defeated in many court cases when they tried to secure their traditional rights. For example, in the so-called Bones Affair in 1839 Norwegians killed a Sámi who was looking at his own traditional lands, but they were freed on the grounds that the murder was considered "self defence". In the legal context, for example, the connection of fishing rights to land ownership openly discriminated against Reindeer Sámi, to the benefit of new colonists. In Guovdageaidnu the Swedish born policeman Bucht was especially known for his anti-Sámi attitude.

The vice of alcohol also originated with Norwegians from south of Sápmi. The colonists, whose experience with agriculture in the northern regions suffered a barren

fate, secured their existence with sidelines: the most profitable was distilling and selling alcohol. Liquor merchants became permanent guests in Sámi siidas and markets. For instance in the 1852 uprising the merchant who was killed was Ruth, a well-known liquor merchant.

It was not necessarily a coincidence that the unrest in Guovdageaidnu in November 1852 happened just a few months after closing of the border between Norway and Finland. It closed the way for the migrating Reindeer Sámi and some of them had to leave their best lichen pastures. The border closing brought great changes for many hundreds of Reindeer Sámi families.

Whereas Laestadius attacked the use of alcohol and other worldly vices, the Guovdageaidnu fanatics went even farther. They wanted to cleanse the whole region of "contamination". The authorities were for them "the devil's children" and Norwegian laws "the devil's doing". Feeling that they had received God's spirit these believers began to feel they were above the law.

The problem was that when Laestadius sternly preached the laws and the Gospels with a double-edged sword of war, the fanatics were not able - in writer Johan Turi's words - to agree if both edges cut the same. According to Turi "the violence of the [religious] laws went to their heads":

Their reason became mixed-up and they began to imitate Laestadius. They preached and passed judgement on anyone who did not follow them. They had their own small group of followers. And later they became even more

Anders Baer (left) and Lars Jacobsen Haetta, sentenced in the Guovdageaidnu Uprising, began to write memoirs about their background and the early stages of Laestadianism. Source: National Board of Antiquities and Historical Monuments, Helsinki.

zealous. They became so irate that they stopped taking care of their lives and began wandering to siidas to preach to Sámi who had heard Laestadius' sermons. But they remembered only to doom to hell all those that did not follow them and begin to preach the same as they did. And when they did not get any more people to join them, they became even more zealous and their reason became muddled even worse."

Into the grip of dominating powers

The first unrest occurred in 1851. The fanatics disrupted the church services in Skiervá and Guovdageaidnu. As the minister turned to kneel at the altar, a certain sectarian mounted the pulpit and began condemning the minister and the dominating powers. In Gáresávvon they threatened to push the small wooden church into the river.

The first event resulted in 22 of the fanatics being sentenced and having to pay for the cost of their transport to prison, as well as the court costs. This was an economic catastrophe for many of them. The border closing did not help the matter at all. The fanatics' anger was more and more directed at the secular powers.

The events of November are shown to have been planned in advance, since at the same time in Gáivuotna a group of fanatics rushed around the market shouting, "The wrath of God has come, burn everything!"

However, in Gáivuotna the authorities suppressed the movement immediately at the beginning by using canons.

Nevertheless, in Guovdageaidnu the fanatics paid a visit to the merchant Ruth and the policeman Bucht, seized and killed them, and set their houses afire. They were content to give the minister Hvoslef a good beating. Before the police and soldiers arrived a group of Sámi came from Ávži village. They managed to calm their compatriots.

Publicly the event was interpreted as an outburst of unorganized, primitive rage, but in the judgement of the case the number of people sentenced and the severity of the punishment told of the seriousness of the "revolt". Five death penalties, three of them commuted to life imprisonment, emphasized the responsibility of the criminals. Twenty-two of the accused received prison sentences, one of them, 18 year old Lars Haetta, was released at age 33.

Ásllat Haetta and Mons Somby, the leaders of the uprising, were executed in 1854. Their bodies were buried outside of the Bossegohppi cemetery. Their skulls were sent to Oslo for anthropological study. They were of scientific interest, in the prejudicial attitudes of the times, for their combined anatomical characteristics of primitive people and criminals. Both skulls were returned and buried in their home communities in the 1990s.

From Siida to Nordic community

Besides the border crossings, other developments in Sámi areas at the end of the 1800s led to the breakdown of the equilibrium of the old Sámi society. As a consequence of these developments the way that the Sámi siidas functioned was finally replaced by the models of the Nordic countries. The Nordic municipal government replaced the centuries old traditional Sámi community. In Norway the local government law of 1837 was a concrete beginning of conscious Norwegianization, as proficiency in the Norwegian language was the main requirement for municipal representatives.

In Finland, municipalities were established beginning in 1865 under the municipality law which imposed municipal governments in the Sámi area by 1893. Here participation in a municipal body was in no way restricted, and therefore many a Sámi became well-known in this sphere.

With the demise of the old system the Sámi tried to look after their own interests in the changing conditions. As the traditional rights of Sámi siidas faded, becoming an agricultural colonist was the only sensible choice for many who had been following a Sámi livelihood. In the northern parts of Finnish Lapland this was clearly seen in the 1800s. When a strong wave of agricultural colonization began in Anár (Aanaar) in the latter part of the 1800s, it was a surprisingly large number of Sámi who brought it about.

The Hunter-fishermen Sámi of Anár (Aanaar) recognized the vanishing of all their fishing waters and hunting grounds through land use conflicts. They had to accept that carrying on with usage from time immemorial was no longer enough. Combined with the diminishing numbers of wild reindeer and declining fish catches, the tax reductions promised to colonists were a strong incentive to become a colonist. Of the farms founded in the last part of the century, 90 percent belonged to Sámi.

Reindeer herding laws were enacted simultaneously in different Nordic countries, but the effect on reindeer herding was strongest in Finland. The reindeer herding legislation in Norway (1883 and 1897) and Sweden (1886 and 1898) was based on the old Sámi siida traditions. In the same way that, in these two countries, Sámi were always accorded special status and treated separately as reindeer herders, under the legislation the right to herd reindeer was given exclusively to Sámi. Only members of Sámi siidas or Sámi could keep reindeer and the reindeer herding area was clearly separated from the agricultural area.

On the Finnish side the legislation concerning reindeer herding was framed differently. The *paliskunta* reindeer herding system, a network of reindeer herding cooperatives, was established by the Finnish administration in 1898. The first actual Reindeer Herding Law went into effect in 1932. The historical situation of reindeer herding was also different than in Norway and Sweden. In Finland, non-Sámi colonists had begun to keep reindeer already in the 1600s. During the spread of reindeer nomadism from Central Scandinavia into Kemi Lapland, the old Giepma Sámi population was largely assimilated by the Finns, who kept the control of reindeer herding in their hands. Within the structure of reindeer herding cooperatives the Sámi area was the smallest part, because the reindeer herding area had reached as far South as Pudasjärvi and Guossan in Finland.

The reindeer herding laws also spelled out the conditions for reindeer herding by Finnish farmers. Reindeer owners were obligated to establish reindeer herding districts with well defined boundaries; certain cooperatives which were bound to precise areas and obligated to certain grazing conditions and other requirements. The administration of these cooperatives is not based on the old kinship or siida communities, but instead on the Finnish model of municipal government. Each cooperative had its own chairman, the "reindeer headman" (Finnish, *poroisäntä*), and its own management board, who were answerable for their local activities to the national government.

The reindeer herding law reflected the situation that the farming mode of reindeer keeping was only a secondary livelihood alongside farming. Reindeer herding areas were not allowed to be separated from agricultural areas, they were to be managed side by side. That led to conflicts between people using different livelihoods, and reindeer herding was often the scapegoat in the eyes of the society oriented toward a farming economy. The

In Norway and Sweden reindeer herding as a secondary livelihood is a special right of the Sámi. Others except Sámi do not have the right to keep reindeer. In Finland others - based on special historic reasons - also can be reindeer herders. In the Sállivárri round-up corral Finns pursue their work with Sámi harmoniously. From left to right Kauko Lehtola, Senja Aikio, Katri Lehtola and Maarit Länsman in the 1950s. Photo: Marja Vuorelainen.

principles of the reindeer herding laws were alien to the traditional Sámi reindeer herding system, resulting in problems in the long run.

The Norwegianization policy

As the old rights of the Sámi siidas became obscure, the benefits of being a colonist clearly began to be emphasized in making decisions. The Sámi no longer had special rights. On the Norwegian side, Sámi benefits began to be consciously trampled upon. After the mid-1800s, in northern Norway, a harsh Norwegianization policy began, which was to last nearly a century. Its most intense period coincided with the general European colonialist period which was strongest from 1870 to 1914.

The Norwegianization policy was partially based on social Darwinist views. Societal relationships were interpreted as a struggle between different sectors of the community. The superiority of European individuals and society was emphasized. This justified developing the "lower" cultures, since they were assumed to be dying.

The power of the Norwegianization policy lay in the fact that it extended into the realm of legal application. The enactment of the Norwegian-oriented legislation was aimed at strengthening Norway's hold over its northern areas, which were strategically important in its relations with Russia. They were directed not only toward Sámi, but just as much toward the coastal Finns, the *Kvens*. The development of the Norwegianization policy can be shown by the chronology of several events:

1851 - Sámi language schools were ordered to function in Norwegian. The schools built and run by Thomas von Westen and Nils V. Stockfleth had managed to exist for 23 years.

1852 - The Norwegian-Russian border was closed, definitely initiated by Russia.

1864 - The first decree on property ownership was based on language competence. Norwegian speakers had priority rights to buy land from the State. The definition of a Norwegian speaker was a person who could speak and read Norwegian. In the same year, the outbreak of the Danish-Prussian war over Schleswig-Holstein caused Denmark to fear that Russia would seize the northern regions. The language ordinance promoted Norwegian colonization in the North.

1871 - The ordinance on Arctic Ocean fishing decreed that foreigners could not own fishing equipment. They could only be assistants to Norwegians. The decree did not yet apply to the border municipalities.

1879 - State lands were designated as Norwegian settlement areas, especially in eastern Finnmark: South Varanger, Unjárga and Tana. Foreign citizens were explicitly forbidden to settle as colonists.

1880 - It was decreed that Sámi and Finnish could only be used in school as a support language. The language of institutions was Norwegian and Norwegianization was promoted in boarding houses connected to schools.

1895 - Free access to land was proclaimed, but again, only for Norwegians. Norwegian citizenship could be gained only if the authorities certified a person's mastery of the Norwegian language.

1897 - Exemption from military service for Sámi and other residents of Finnmark was repealed. Now everyone 21 years of age had to do military service. Norway thus rescinded, at one blow, both the old Sámi siidas' traditional right to exemption from taxation, as well as from military service that had been guaranteed by the Strömstad Treaty. The first military exercises were held in Áltá in the summer of 1898. The first Sámi soldier was Ole Anders Eira. (Russia rescinded the Sámi right to exemption from the army in 1915, and Finland in 1919.)

1898 - A law was passed forbidding the use of Sámi language in schools in Sápmi.

1902 - The law on land ownership was made more specific. It connected ownership more firmly to language by assigning a Norwegian name to properties. These names later became family surnames.

1902 - The use of interpreters was forbidden in administrative institutions.

1905 - The teaching and use of Sámi language in the Romsa (Tromsa) seminary was forbidden. Connected to this, an attempt was made to attract Norwegian speaking teachers to Sápmi by offering special salaries.

Two main trends can be distinguished in the measures employed in the Norwegianization policy. The first was settlement and economic policy, aimed at establishing Norwegian agricultural colonization and farming, above all in the eastern parts of the Sámi area. The second was language and education policy aimed at eradicating the Sámi lan-

In different countries there were varying strategies toward Sámi assimilation. It was hardest in Norway where the language policy specially strove to make proper Norwegians out of 'Lapps'. The use of Sámi was forbidden in schools and boarding houses.

guage from schools and from the seminary. Speaking Sámi was forbidden in student boarding houses. An added factor was the law on purchasing land that linked ownership to language proficiency.

There were many trends in the Norwegianization policy. Through *active* colonialism: Sámi were clearly to be assimilated into Norwegian society and they were to obliterate the Sámi language. According to Johan Sverdrup "The only way to save the 'Lapps' is for them to merge into the Norwegian People". Through *implied* colonialism: it was possible the Sámi could become civilized by converting to Christianity and by reading general refined literature in Sámi. By civilizing the Sámi it would be possible to direct them into the Norwegian language and culture.

The century old methods of Norwegianization permeated the work of many a government and many a committee. Not until 1953 did the Romsa (Tromsa) Seminary again begin to teach in Sámi. The Norwegian language statute from 1898 was repealed in 1959. Even after that, the negative attitudes towards Sámi culture and language persisted for a long time.

In Sweden the relations with Sámi took their own form, called the segregation and isolation policy. It was seemingly more moderate than Norway's but resembled a policy of implied assimilation. It was based on an awareness of the distinctness of Sámi as a group. In the time of King Karl IX, Sámi had already been seen as specialists in certain fields and their rights needed to be secured for the benefit of the State. This was done by keeping them clearly confined and separated from the colonists.

The stereotype of Sámi as reindeer herders living free in the fells took shape toward the end of the 1800s with the idea "A Lapp must remain a Lapp". Due to this image, the reindeer herding Sámi were kept patronizingly far from all the demoralizing effects of "civilization". They were not supposed to settle in permanent places, for example, because in the opinion of the authorities they would neglect their herding.

A separate school system was created for Sámi, especially for reindeer herders: the nomad schools. Sámi children were supposed to be able to grow up in the "genuine" environment. Nevertheless the language of the schools was often Swedish. The emphasis put on reindeer herding caused other Sámi to attend these schools, although this educational innovation had not been intended for them. Also, the reindeer herding laws magnified the differences among the Sámi groups because reindeer herding and being Sámi were combined unofficially more and more.

The ideas of social Darwinism reached Finland later than elsewhere in the Nordic countries, not until the 1920s and 1930s. The reason was Finland's independence in 1917, when it needed to seek its own identity as a state. Research that aimed at building and promoting the Finnish national identity began to draw distinct borders versus Russians and Swedes, and in addition versus "primitive" peoples like the Sámi, who were culturally related.

Awakening of Sápmi

With the strengthening of the ruling population's grip, and the weakening of their own livelihoods, the Sámi began to understand the significance of pan-Sámi national cooperation. The separate local organizations turned towards more general encompassing Sámi viewpoints. The name *Sápmi* (Land of the Sámi) began to be held up as a general concept, especially when parts of the Land of the Sámi were being broken into pieces regionally.

There is no evidence of incidents of Sámi aggressive resistance in history. Therefore, the Guovdageaidnu riot is interpreted as an uprising by the Sámi as a people, although its origins were primarily religious. In the same way the "first awakening" of the Sámi in the early 1900s was more a mounting reaction to local conditions of narrowing circumstances of existence rather than a real recognition of an overall Sámi identity.

The counter-reaction arose generally out of friction and conflict between the Sámi and the colonists over the zone along the Lapland Border and the southern parts of Sápmi. The first organization was illustrative; the South Sámi *Fatmomakka* Association (later called the Wilhelmina-Åsele Sámi Association) was founded in 1904. It was born against the background of conflicts with colonists over the hay lands of the region. Through the association's leadership and activities the conflict over settlement in the river valley finally was resolved so that both reindeer herders and farmers were able to get along together.

In its statutes, the association stressed its attempt to improve the societal, economic and political position of the Sámi. Its leader was a powerful woman - Elsa Laula. She became known through an outspoken book in defence of the Sámi, *Inför lif eller död?* (Life or Death?), in which she denounced the Swedes' penetration across the Lapland Border to colonize, and drew attention to the importance of Sámi cooperation. Laula was ferociously attacked in the Swedish press for her opinions. Likewise, representatives of the association were reprimanded for their activities by the governor of the province of Västerbotten.

Pressure from the association caused the State to establish nomad schools and a state committee to look into Sámi affairs, although not in the best possible ways: the committee was "manned" with Swedes, and the schools were mainly taught in Swedish. In addition to Laula, another leading figure was the versatile Torkel Tomasson.

In Norway, five local organizations were founded between 1906 and 1908, all in the southern parts of Sápmi. In the 1910s Sámi organizations began to be established in Finnmark in Norway, as well. The enthusiasm for creating organizations is shown by the fact that, in 1920, when the Sámi Central Association was founded in Sweden, it had nine local member organizations.

The peak of Sámi social activism was the gen-

At the beginning of the 1900s the South Sámi, Elsa Laula, was a powerful woman during social unrest. As a writer and speaker she took a strong position towards matters concerning the Sámi.

eral meeting of Sámi held in Trondheim, Norway, on February 6, 1917. It was the first attempt to gather Sámi representatives across borders; this was also highlighted in the presentations. "Today we try for the first time to unite Sámi from Norway and Sweden", Elsa Laula-Renberg declared at the opening. Mostly South Sámi participated in the meeting. The day of that meeting is now the Sámi national day.

Still more extensive was the four-day meeting held a year later in Östersund, Sweden, in February 1918, which was attended by more than 200 Sámi from both Norway and Sweden. The main focus of the meeting was to break the popular attitudes of the Swedes according to which Sámi culture could not renew itself "unspoiled". In the opinion of the meeting, the attitude in education and economic life, "A Lapp must remain a Lapp", must not be allowed to result in Sámi being excluded from all sorts of enriching cultural pursuits. The meeting demanded for reindeer herders the possibility of permanent residences and more regular schooling. At the same time they emphasized that Sámi must not be distinguished on the basis of economic activity, but all Sámi should be recognized.

Alongside these organizational activities Sámi publishing came into being. The first Sámi language newspaper *Nuorttanaste* (Eastern Star, est. 1898) is still published today; it was basically a religious paper. In contrast, *Sagai Muittalægje* (The News Reporter), begun on the Norwegian side in 1904, presented a narrow Sámi political editorial policy. The paper, founded and edited by Sea Sámi Anders Larsen, had a strong nationalistic, preaching as well as enlightening tone.

This newspaper published informative, political and literary texts. One of Larsen's most successful projects was to support teacher Isak Saba to be elected to the Norwegian Storting (National Parliament), where he was active as the only Sámi from 1908 to 1912. The newspaper died after seven years of publication.

Even shorter-lived was its contemporary, *Lapparnas Egen Tidning* (The Sámi's Own Newspaper), which appeared on the Swedish side in 1904-1905. It tried to promote improved school conditions, democracy in local government, temperance and work in cultural education. According to the newspaper the Sámi "will win in the struggle against an ice-cold cultural death". Daniel Mortenson's paper *Waren Sardne* (Fell Conversations, 1910-1913, 1922-1925) directed its attention to the legal position of reindeer herding Sámi.

Other more enduring papers were born, besides *Nuorttanaste*. Tomasson founded, in 1919, the *Samefolkets Egen Tidning* (The Sámi People's Own Newspaper), later *Samefolket* (The Sámi People), which presented a wide range of cultural ideas. Tomasson's concept was a key issue in Sámi politics at the time. "The cultural movement of the Sámi people is a social and spiritual movement that has subversive influence to break with the old dogmas, delusions and one-sided views of the existence and development of the Sámi people. The same movement, in positive opinions, is the stage in the Sámi people's awakening to realize their position as a community - with it the enlightenment and promotion of the awakening has to come from the people themselves."

Writers were an integral part of the Sámi "awakening". Although in their work, Johan Turi, Pedar Jalvi, and Anders Larsen depicted the situation in Sápmi each in their own way, they also created new concepts of Sámi thought and self-image - for outsiders and for the Sámi themselves. Through literary means they tried to awaken Sámi to the recognition of their own uniqueness.

The general national Sámi spirit was declared directly in literary texts. Isak Saba, revered as the Sámi national poet, wrote the national anthem of Sápmi, which he ended with the emphatic exclamation, *"Sámeeatnan sámiide!"* (Sápmi for the Sámi!). Fjellner's idea of "the sons of the sun" as well as Saba's exclamation have found a reverberating echo only in modern times.

In the part of Sápmi that is in Finland, organizational activities did not begin in the early 1900s. The *Lapin Sivistysseura* (Society for the Promotion of Lapp Culture) was founded by Finnish friends of Lapland in 1932. The first of the Sámis' own organizations *Samii Litto* (Sámi Alliance) was founded during the evacuation to Central Ostrobothnia in 1945.

Sagai Muittalægje

1as April 1906.

No. 7.

Same soga laula.

...

Isak Saba.

Stuoradigge-valljim.

...

Sagai Muittaleagje (left) was the first Sámi political newspaper. It influenced the election of Isak Saba (right) as the first Sámi member to the Storting in Norway.

PIONEERS OF SÁMI LITERATURE

Sámi literature truly emerges in the 1900s and began to flower in the 1970s. At the beginning of the 20th century there were several pioneering writers of note. In their writings the same themes can be seen that are still in Sámi writings of the last decade. They stressed the importance of the Sámi language in conveying people's experience of the world; they dealt in depth with the position of Sámi within a foreign society; and they portrayed Sámi - especially youth - surrendering their Sámi identity.

"They were at home..."

The teacher-journalist-writer from Kárášjohka Matti Aikio (1872-1929) was, in the true sense, the first Sámi writer, but he wrote in Norwegian. A problem familiar to many Sámi and Sámi writers is crystallized in Aikio. For a long time he tried to deny his Sámi identity and find Germanic blood in himself - at one point he even supported the Norwegianization policy. Nevertheless, he wrote about Sámi themes, and later in his life he was ready to side with his own people.

Aikio's perception is quite consistent and descriptive. He was the first Sámi in Norway to graduate from high school, studying from 1894 to 1896, during the time of the most severe Norwegianization policy. Growing up in a Sámi speaking family, Aikio struggled long to learn the Norwegian language properly. He went on to the provincial teachers' college in Čáhcesuolu, though he still spoke Norwegian poorly. Attempting the teacher's seminary in Romsa (Tromsø) two years later, he studied

Sámi as a second subject. He later declared,

"If only I could have written in Sámi. It is hard to write in a language that is not one's own. I noticed that at school. They laughed at me, the others did. I knew that I was not worse than others. But I became nervous and unsure. I noticed that I could not trust myself. Their ears were accustomed and they had the instincts to proceed. They were at home. I was a stranger."

Aikio's feeling of inferiority because of being Sámi grew intense over the years. His reaction was typical: he wanted to deny his background. He wrote to a Sámi acquaintance, "You will not become anything because you are a 'Lapp'. I will become something because I am Germanic!" Also, the world which Aikio tried to invade as a noteworthy artist looked at him condescendingly and in a racist manner. He was mocked as a drunken "Lapp" and called "Boccaccio Borealis".

This turmoil is seen in Aikio's works. In the first three works he struggles to be free of the bonds of race. In the book *I Dyreskinn* (In Animal Hides, 1906) he portrays the collision of cultural modes between the coastal community and the protagonist's orientation towards the Norwegian merchant family. He describes the position of the minority in an aggressive society, also setting the subject in another group, Jews.

Later Aikio's views became better understood by Sámi. In his last work he attacked the assimilation policies. In an interview before his death he said, "If only I had been able to write in Sámi ..."

Prophets in their own lands

The fate of Johan Turi (1854-1936) from Čohkkiras fulfilled the old rule: a poor, talented storyteller creates immortal literature by freeing himself from the demands of daily chores. That is what happened when Hjalmar Lundholm, the director of the Kiruna mine, became the writer's patron and the Dane Emilie Demant began working as his secretary and housekeeper.

Unlike Aikio, who used literary realism, the Sámi speaking writer Johan Turi saw his mission primarily to inform and to preserve information. Turi had experienced the curses of agricultural colonization as well as of the national border agreements. In his view, the conflicts between the Sámi and the colonists stemmed from the fact that outsiders did not understand Sámi life and way of thinking.

Just relating "all about Sámi life and conditions" Turi wrote the book *Muittalus samid birra* (in Sámi and Danish, 1910: Memoirs of a Sámi; English version "Turi's Book of Lapland", 1912). His writing style is both literary and documentary. He approaches Sámi culture from inside, its oral tradition, heritage and stories.

Turi's style follows in the footsteps of the old narratives. His sentences move "strung out like a long string of reindeer" - along the terrain. Turi's explanations are precise, the words a delight. Best remembered are the detailed accuracy of reindeer matters, the eagerness to remember fables, and the cunning irony that emerges as an enormous fable at the conclusion of the book "in the tale about the unknown animals of Lapland".

Turi lived a simple life even as a well-known author, whose works were translated into Danish, German, Swedish, and English during his lifetime. He made several trips, one of which, to the North, he wrote about in the small book *Från fjället* (From the Fells). In his later days he developed a livelihood as a tourist trap; he made and sold to tourists pictures of Sámi themes, which he produced "industrially" by stamping.

Programmatic literature

Where Turi saw his mission to record information for the common memory, Anders Larsen (1870-1949) in Norway and Pedar Jalvi (1888-1916) in Finland envisioned their task as writers to awaken their own people to take a look at themselves and at the dangers threatening Sámi. Between 1904 and 1911 Larsen was editor of *Sagai Muittalægje*, a magazine which published short literary pieces. When the magazine folded, he compiled his work *Beavvi-Alggo* (Dawn, 1912). The book is sharply critical and realistic, but through its melodramatic twists it gives a picture of Sámi youth growing up in a foreign language environment.

Jalvi, from the Deatnu valley, scattered his powers in many quarters during his short lifetime. In a single volume *Muottačalmit* (Snowflakes, 1915) he tried to show the beauty of Sámi as a literary language and through that bring a "breath of light" to the Sámi. The work is a collection of poems and short tales on various subjects.

The literary tradition begun by Larsen and Jalvi can be called programmatic literature. They understood the value of literature for identity; it could perhaps entice

Johan Turi from Čohkkiras was a member of a Reindeer Sámi family who came from Guovdageaidnu. Nonetheless he had lost all his reindeer and was known for his Bohemian life style. He was a writer as well as a painter.

Sámi to see themselves and their culture as an important matter bearing their own stamp. Their works are unfinished and sometimes even raw, because the primary goal of their literary output was not psychological credibility or stylistic sophistication, just the Sámi national message. Polemics and taking sides were typical of the programmatic literature which experienced a new wave in the 1970s.

Another man from the Deatnu, Hans-Aslak Guttorm (1907-1991), did his part to develop Sámi as a literary language. He believed that only Sámi could capture the life of Sámi and their characteristic way of thinking because Sámi have internalized these through their language. In his book *Koccam spalli* (The Rising Gust of Wind, 1941) Guttorm penetrated the whole Sámi way of life through the language. In the short stories about the daily life of people living on the Deatnu he combined poetry with reality. The work, which he had to shorten because of difficulties in publication, also included many classic poems.

51

Wartime as a turning point

World War II was the first time in history that Sámi, a peaceful people, were called up by the Soviet Union, Norway and Finland to be soldiers. During six years of war Sámi experienced the whole irony of fighting a war. In the Finnish-Soviet Winter War of 1939-40 Finland's Sámi fought against invading Soviet forces in which Kola Sámi were also fighting. In the spring of 1940 Sámi in Norway fought alongside allied forces against the invading German army.

Only one year later Finland's Sámi were supporting the Germans to attack the Soviet Union, whose forces still included Kola Sámi. In theory it was possible that Sámi fired at each other at the Petsamo (Peäccam) front. During the occupation of Norway Sámi were participants in the resistance units that sabotaged the Germans. Finally in 1944-45, Sámi fought alongside Finnish troops against the withdrawing Germans, who burned practically all of Sápmi in Finland and Norway.

Finland's Continuation War against the Soviet Union began in June 1941 and ended in early September 1944, but according to the armistice Finland had to begin fighting against the German army, which withdrew towards its base areas in northern Norway. The whole civil population in Finnish Lapland was evacuated from the war zone. The Finnish authorities carried out the evacuation very carefully.

The situation on the Norwegian side was different. Because there the evacuation was ordered and overseen by the German army, which had occupied Norway since May 1940, the population reacted negatively. Many people decided to try to remain in their home region without official permission. Forced evacuation along the main routes or close to the coast succeeded better. In spite of that, many inhabitants living inland spent the winter hidden in the fells, forests or mountains. Almost one third of the 72,000 inhabitants that were to be evacuated remained "spending the winter" in their home regions.

The German troops burned the Province of Lapland in Finland and the provinces of northern Norway including Sápmi as they retreated, especially along the main roads. In general, the far-ther North in Finnish Lapland, the greater the destruction was. Eanodat and Anár (Aanaar) municipalities were 80 to 90 percent destroyed. Ohcejohka municipality, where travel was more difficult, was largely spared the devastation. Likewise, northern Norway was destroyed at the coast and in large centres, while in the remote areas at least some buildings survived.

The destruction of centuries old settlements meant an interruption in material culture. That was accentuated by reconstruction. The roads brought large numbers of people to participate in the reconstruction of these areas. Sápmi began to become greatly changed through the influence of outsiders, Finns and Norwegians.

In Finland, in the fringes of the Sámi region Finnish type settlements like Ivalo were developed; for example, Gáregasnjárga's residential zone originated along the highway after the war. The post office, police station, frontier guard barracks and health services became possible largely because of the improved roads - and the language of all these institutions was Finnish.

The reconstruction in Sápmi took place entirely in the Finnish manner, with standard Finnish style houses. Likewise Finnish ideals began to be seen in the daily life and habits of Sámi. The clearest sign of the new influences was the change in clothing; Sámi garments started to be replaced by Finnish clothing. Part of the reason was that Finnish clothing was easily obtainable, but it was also a question of fashion.

New Finnish implements and ornaments began to appear in Sámi households. Sámi started to go to dances and visit other places where the Sámi language was not welcome. Even Santa Claus, who had no meaning for Sámi, made official visits to the Deatnu after the war. The Finnish influence could also be seen in local government in Sápmi. Up until the 1950s, Sámi was the language of the Ohcejohka municipal council, but now it changed to Finnish, although the council still had a Sámi majority.

The most important economic influences brought by the evacuation was the breakthrough of tilling and cultivating the land, for instance, along the Deatnu. That caused the very rapid disappearance of the old Sámi network of summer

In Ohcejohka Finnicization was rapid after the war. Before the war the language in meetings was Sámi, as in this picture of the municipal committee on income and property taxes taken by E. N. Manninen in the 1930s. Two decades later Finnish was the language in meetings, although the majority of their members was Sámi. Source: Eila Lahti's archive.

places. Gathering hay from natural meadows and collecting lichen for reindeer gradually stopped. The development of cultivated meadows for hay-dairy farming, as well as wage employment, required workers to establish permanent residences.

Along with the ideals of a cash economy, this led to the demise of the Sámi economic base. Cash began to have a meaning among Sámi, underlined by working for wages: they began to buy finished products, no longer preparing them much at home. Divided into different economic segments, Sámi no longer saw the way of life that followed seasonal migrations as being "effective"; but to secure monetary benefits they thought it best to concentrate on one economic activity only. Following the Finnish values, that activity was farming, the omnipotence of which was idealized in Finnish Lapland in comparison to reindeer herding.

Perhaps the largest element in the assimilation of Sámi in Finland was the school system. In 1946 a law making school attendance mandatory abolished the use of the long-standing catechist educational system in which teachers skilled in a Sámi language travelled around to teach pupils who lived dispersed in Sápmi. The law obliged residents of remote areas to send their children to central schools. Collecting them in large school centres and boarding houses, combined with instruction given in Finnish and stressing Finnish cultural values, estranged Sámi children from their own background and culture.

Despite the negative changes, in Sámi opinion the wartime brought positive consequences as well. The general attitudes towards Sámi changed their human dignity, and the rights of small minorities were emphasized due to international developments.

FROM THE FENS OF SÁPMI TO THE LOWLANDS OF OSTROBOTHNIA

The order to evacuate came to Sápmi in Finland on very short notice. It reached some Deatnu valley people far away in the mountain birch forests when they were stacking hay in swampy natural meadows. Returning home, the hay makers met the villagers already set to leave, with their necessities in their laps and hands, the rest of their belongings buried in the ground. Peäccam (Beahcán), Anár, and Ohcejohka municipalities were in the first zone of urgency, and the inhabitants were to leave on September 7, 1944 without delay.

One of the conditions in the armistice between the Soviet Union and Finland was the demand that the German troops be removed from Finland by mid September. Because the time allowed was definitely too short for the Germans to pull out 200 000 men and all the equipment from an area between Oulu in the South to Petsamo (Peäccam) in the North, war between Finland and Germany became unavoidable.

The evacuation of the sparsely populated Sámi area in little more than one week was a great achievement for the Finnish authorities and the residents alike. People had to be collected nearly one by one from the huge expanse of Sápmi in distant areas accessible only by boat or on foot. From the collection points, the evacuees were taken to Rovaniemi by truck.

Ninety percent of the trucks were German. The German vehicles were constantly transporting equipment northward, and the German commanding officer in Ivalo, on his own initiative, had given orders that they were not to return empty - without evacuees - to Rovaniemi.

Despite the suddenness of the departure, Sámi did not appear to panic. Heikki Sarre from Aanaar crystallized the calm mood, stating while drawing on his pipe, "isn't it great that even the children get to see a little of the world".

The problems for refugees

In all, around two thousand Sámi evacuees were counted in Finland. Most of them were evacuated to central Ostrobothnia. Those from Aanaar were placed in Ylivieska, from Ohcejohka in Alavieska; Skolt Sámi were taken to Kalajoki and the small Soabbat Sámi population to Himanka. Only 250 Reindeer Sámi from Eanodat went to the Swedish side. Central Ostrobothnia was the closest safe area for relocation, since the front line between the Finns and the Germans was at the level of Oulu.

There had been no time to plan evacuation locations, and for many municipalities receiving the northern refugees, in addition to the refugees from Karelia, which had been ceded to the Soviet Union by Finland, became a great burden. It was no wonder that there were difficulties adjusting from time to time. When the Sámi, a natural people from the North, travelled to a completely different culture, among typical Finnish farmers, familiar problems arose for many of the refugees.

The lifestyle and values of the Finnish peasants were far removed from the Sámi way of life close to nature. For example, the Skolt Sámi, whose lifestyle was one of annual migrations, had habits and perceptions of cleanliness that did not meet the standards appropriate in a permanent dwelling. Relations were in other ways mostly negative toward the Skolt Sámi, who were Russian orthodox and influenced by Russian culture. On some level the Sámi from Anár (Aanaar) and Ohcejohka, who practised some farming and spoke a little Finnish, seemed closer to the new setting.

Because of the speed of the evacuation, the Sámi were not able to be introduced to the Ostrobothnians in the best possible way. The Sámi had no equipment nor food, and their arrival at the busiest time in the autumn could not have been pleasant. There were prejudices on both sides. For example, in some Deatnu areas "peasants", a derogatory term for Finns, were generally feared and thought to be crazy or murderers, because a Finn who accidentally arrived in one place had killed his family while mentally disturbed.

Over the course of the winter the prejudices subsided, and the Ostrobothnians developed better relations with many Sámi than with, for example, the Karelians. However, there were enough difficulties during the evacuation, some stemming from the sullenness of the local people, some from the problems of taking care of the refugees. Naturally they had to live together in very cramped conditions, which prompted the wish of some host families to save their best rooms from the "dirty" evacuees. The food situation in Ostrobothnia was already difficult, and when rations and food coupons ran out the only resource was often the black market, which also took what little money they had.

The change in diet, the coastal climate, and the Sámi's lack of immunity to southern illnesses meant that there were many more deaths among evacuated Sámi than among the local people. The death bells already began to ring in the first weeks. During the winter children especially died from stomach illnesses and infectious diseases: diphtheria, whooping cough and typhoid.

"Better not to complain"

Disregarding the difficulties and longing for home, the Sámi adjusted to the circumstances. In situations that they could not influence they adopted an attitude of accommodation. Karl Nickul declared that no matter which direction the conditions turned, rain or shine, a Sámi would happen to say, "That's alright, too", or "It is fine - better not to complain."

Many older Sámi remember the evacuation period very favourably - it brought new, unforgettable experiences aplenty. Living through a winter in a community of Finnish farmers was an immense cultural transition for the Sámi - a whole new world. Many of them had never before been outside their own municipalities.

Highways, cars, railways and trains were wonders many had never seen. While the arrivals were used to seeing in their home regions two to three cows in a barn, now under one roof there could be forty needing to be milked. Everything was huge. A Sámi family's home could have fit in the living room of an Ostrobothnian farmhouse. Turnip and grain fields reached far toward the horizon.

"New kinds of animals" were discovered every day, like on a research expedition. The boys from the Lower Deatnu thought chickens

In the spring and summer of 1945, when the Sámi returned to their home regions, they found them destroyed. Only in remote regions were buildings saved from burning by the Germans.

were a Siberian bird and hunted them for eating. The pigs grunting in the sties were strange to many northern residents. The Skolt Sámi had seen them before the war when an army officer brought ten pigs to Peäccam as an experiment. The Skolt, nevertheless, had killed and eaten them as seals, wondering only at their strange colour.

Of course, too much emphasis should not be put on the splendours of Ostrobothnia. The desolation and flat expanses of the Ostrobothnian lowlands began to oppress the dwellers from the fells. Muddy water was shocking to the evacuees, who were used to clear water lakes and rivers. Even the standard of living of the Ostrobothnians was not in itself better than that of the Reindeer Sámi or Laplanders used to the "Lapland bonus" paid in the Province of Lapland.

Although the major military skirmishes of the Lapland War

ended in November 1944, the evacuees from the northernmost municipalities were only allowed to return the following spring and summer - some even later - because of the hazards of mines. Returning to their homes, the Sámi evacuees faced ashes and coals; chimneys sticking out like skeletons were reminders of their ruined homes. To begin a new life, they created hurriedly put together huts, potato cellars, dugout shelters and cardboard shacks.

Beginning a new life amid the devastation of Sápmi was difficult. In addition to the destroyed buildings the loose possessions were stolen or destroyed. The destruction of their boats was fatal for the Fishing Sámi, as was the destruction of reindeer for the Reindeer Sámi. For Sámi, the period of reconstruction completed the development that had begun during the evacuation.

The flag became an important symbol of the new Sámi movement. It was first hoisted during the Áltá Conflict; the present design combining colours in a circle signifying unity was approved at the Sámi Conference in 1986. Parade of the City Sámi on Sámi National Day in Helsinki in 1993. Photo: Jorma Lehtola.

PARTICIPANTS IN MODERN SOCIETY

The entry of Sápmi into modern society has improved conditions and standard of living, but it has, as well, caused a crisis in traditional Sámi society. Technological advances have changed livelihoods and communications. Modern permanently settled way of life has brought about changes in living habits. Formal education and adapting to the larger society's structure informs one's view of the world.

The crisis is not the first one for the Sámi, but it is stronger and more penetrating. Sámi culture no longer can absorb influences in peace as it did before. The assimilation and adaptation process now invades even spiritual life. While attending schools run by the majority society and taught in a foreign language, Sámi adopt the values of the Nordic countries and often become estranged from their own background.

This situation has also caused a backlash. Improved communications and information networks have, together with pressure from outside, led to a growing feeling of solidarity among Sámi. There is a consciousness that all Sámi once again form a community, Sápmi, which the national borders and other historical events had destroyed.

The birth of an ethnic identity was only possible when the family and village based local identity of Sámi culture was exchanged for a general Sámi identity, a general Sámi feeling of belonging. A village and group identity changed to a feeling of ethnic community and solidarity.

The development of this feeling came in waves and was different in each region in the different countries. Sámi awareness of their own solidarity developed in the postwar years when fumbling attempts at alliance turned into a fighting attitude. It climaxed when Sámi from the different countries joined in the demonstration against the damming of the Álta River in 1980-81. This identity is built on many different levels; Sámi politics overlap culture, media development overlaps national identity, and art, the feeling of community.

The process of developing an identity can be seen in the way the words naming Sámi (Finnish: saamelainen, Swedish and Norwegian: same, Russian: saamskii) gradually displaced the old name "Lapp" (lappalainen, lapp, lopari). It was not a matter of taking on a new ideology, but the viewpoint had changed. In place of attitudes from outside in the majority population's public opinion, the Sámi's own image of themselves emerged - out of their own culture. It was based on the age-old word that appears in all Sámi languages, past and present, the present day North Sámi sápmelaš. The minority, an aboriginal people, was claiming the right to define its own public image.

The word Sámi had been used in Finnish already in the early 1900s, and in other Scandinavian languages in the 1800s and even earlier, but it was only after the war that it began to be used as a clear expression of the Sámi's own voice. They used it consistently in the names of Sámi organizations, activities and committees on Sámi affairs.

On the Norwegian side there were the organizations Sámi Sær'vi and Oslo Sámi Sær'vi (1948), in Sweden Same-Ätnam (1945) and Samii Litto (1945) in Finland. In Finland the Samii Litto used that name in their own records, but for official communications they consistently used the Finnish word for Sámi, saamelainen, such as in the report of the Sámi Affairs Committee (Saamelaisasiain komitean mietintö) issued in 1952. Outside Sámi society the word "Lapp" remained in general use until the 1970s and 1980s, and in some places into the 1990s.

Changing Sápmi and the Sámi movement

The international re-examination of human rights after World War II, which had been fuelled by its abuses, made it impossible to carry on with the accustomed nationalistic attitudes. In the atmosphere of changing ideology, ideas about the value of individuals and the rights of small peoples and minorities improved so that the United Nations added an important section to its Charter securing serious attention for the priority of aboriginal peoples' rights.

The United Nations Declaration of Human Rights stressed the rights of different groups and their members. Samuli Aikio states that by entering into new agreements and resolutions, the Nordic countries began to re-examine their attitude toward their national minorities. The new attitudes, along with scientific research, overturned the racially prejudiced images of Sámi that had been widely presented and publicized before the war. However, these good intentions often did not translate into actions, which were dictated by the economic and social realities of rebuilding after the war, especially in Norway and Finland.

The Sámi's own national thinking developed very slowly until the 1960s. Their own cultural groups had little feeling of belonging together. The drawing of the borders demarcating the four countries where the Sámi live ultimately caused divisions of culture and language among the Sámi where there had been none before. The first Sámi associations in Norway and Sweden very clearly limited the respective Sámi group to activities within the given country. The importance of cooperation among individual activists continued as before.

Characteristic of the way that Sámi found their common identity was the founding of the first Sámi association in Finland immediately after the war. Before the war the four Sámi groups in Finland lived independently of one another. Toward the end of the war the Sámi were all evacuated to Central Ostrobothnia. During this evacuation period, while living together in communities of Finnish farmers who spoke a foreign language and had strange customs, they realized the existence of a "Sámi people" who had similar clothing and thinking patterns, and spoke a similar language.

The loss of their homes, the feeling of insecurity and strangeness opened a new social realm which promoted the strengthening of the feeling of belonging together. It led to the birth of an organization, *Samii Litto* (Sámi Alliance), founded at Easter 1945 in Central Ostrobothnia. This was the Sámi's answer to the Lapin Sivistysseura, the Finnish organization for people sympathetic to Sámi and founded in Helsinki in 1932.

In Sweden the organization *Riikasearvi Sáme Ätnam* (RSÄ) (The National Association of Sápmi) was founded in 1945. Its long-time chair was Professor Israel Ruong, himself of partial Sámi descent. *Sámiid Riikasearvi / Svenska Samernas Riksförbund* (SR/SSR) (Sámi National Association of Sweden) was founded in 1950. The *Norgga Boazosápmelaččaid Riikkasearvi* (NBR) (Sámi Reindeer Herders' Association of Norway) was founded in 1948, and the Sámi living in the capital created the local organization *Oslo Sami Sær'vi* (Oslo Sámi Society).

It was not until later that the next local associations appeared with the *Kárášjohka Sámi Sær'vi* (Kárášjohka Sámi Society) in 1956 and the *Guovdageaidnu Sámi Sær'vi* (Guovdageaidnu Sámi Society) in 1963. In Finland the only similar local association was the *Ohcejohka Sámi Siida* founded in 1959. It had great significance as the organ of Sámi cooperation in Finland's only municipality with a Sámi majority. In 1998 the *Suoma Sámiid Guovddášsearvi* (SSG) (Finland's Central Association of Sámi) was founded.

Samii Litto had a great impact on the Finnish government's establishment of a committee to draw up a plan for the development of Sámi affairs. In their report (1952) the committee made progressive, and even some radical, proposals. Particular attention and opposition from authorities was raised by the idea of special Sámi areas where Sámi privileges and rights in their actual areas of occupancy would be protected. The committee's work was largely ignored and never implemented.

The Norwegian Sámi Committee Report was prepared at the end of the 1950s. It was one of the first noteworthy attempts to examine the issues of Sámi culture and administration, but again its prac-

Three prominent Sámi figures during the post-war period in Finland. Johan Nuorgam (upper left) was the initiator of the Sámi radio and the chair of the association *Samii Litto*. A significant achievement was the establishment of the Anár Sámi Museum. Matti Sverloff (lower left) was the long-time 'person of trust' (headman) of the Skolt Sámi. Pekka Lukkari (right), teacher and principal, took an active part in pan-Nordic Sámi politics from the beginning and was a member of the first Sámediggi in Finland.

tical implementation was not followed up. One reform in Norway was the repeal in 1959 of a law from 1898 promoting Norwegianization and forbidding the use of Sámi in schools in the Sámi area in Norway.

At first, teaching materials in Sámi languages and teachers were available from the teachers' college in Romsa (Tromsa), which had taught Sámi since 1953. Later many other regional Sámi teachers' colleges came into existence. In Kárášjohka and Guovdageaidnu, after the war, Sámi operated their own "nomadic Sámi classes" among reindeer herders. Together with a number of other schools founded by Sámi in other places these were primary schools responding to Sámi interests. In 1958 a Sámi high school was opened in Guovdageaidnu.

A milestone in modern Sámi history is 1953, when the first Sámi Conference was held in Johkamohkki, Sweden. The organizers were the sister associations *Sami Sær'vi*, Lapin Sivistysseura and *Same-Åtnam*. It was characteristic that a minority of the participants at this first conference were Sámi; they gave only seven of the twenty seven presentations. Israel Ruong, the chair for Same-Åtnam, drew a clear picture of the situation which set Sámi politics into motion.

"The Sámi of the Nordic countries are a small minority and a distinct culture with its roots deep in nature and in the history of the North. Modern development, especially the expansion of technology into Lapland, has thrust this ethnic group into a difficult situation. In order to preserve the culture's distinctiveness their adaptation to the new times must be highly active. Active adaptation means that Sámi can not alone and without criticism adopt modern culture, casting aside their culture's irreplaceable values, but that they hold fast to their cultural traditions in the new conditions. Active adaptation must include, among other things, that Sámi wakefully follow every change in the new situation and themselves signal what touches Sámi cultural research and advantages ..."

Ethnologist Phebe Fjellström has regarded this statement as an expression of a change in attitude, from passive to active, in regard to issues. The Conference emphasized the importance of Sámi rights with respect to natural resources and language. In addition, it stressed the role of Sámi language education in the preservation of the whole culture.

The significance of the conference was to highlight the reality that issues that had been viewed as separate questions and problems were now seen as a whole complex combining economic policies, language research, identity and languages. It was clear that this holistic view also implied a feeling of community among Sámi through a pan-Nordic identity.

The most important result of the Conference was the founding in 1956 of Sámiráđđi (Sámi Council). The Sámi of the Kola Peninsula in Russia joined the Sámiráđđi in 1991. From the beginning it drew attention to securing Sámi immemorial usage rights. The Sámiráđđi's most visible manifestations have been the Sámi Conferences that they organize every third year.

The Sámi Delegation to Helsinki in 1947. Seated from the right: Nilla Outakoski, Jaakko Keränen, Nillo Magga and Leo Karppinen. Standing from the right: Karl Nickul, Matti Sverloff, Erkki Jomppanen and an unknown person. Source: Erkki Nickul's archive.

The initiators of the Sámi Museum in Anár - (from left) Erkki Jomppanen, Johan Nuorgam and Juhani Jomppanen - greet a Finn or a donor. Photo: Teuvo Lehtola.

Sámi decision-makers kept relations with their counterparts and news media in the South. The old generation's protagonist Juhani Jomppanen (in front) and the young politician Erkki Jomppanen at the Finnish press centre in Helsinki in 1950. Source: Piera Jomppanen's archive.

Schools and boarding houses

Despite progressive steps in using active cultural policies, the situation in the 1960s was still somewhat controversial. Many Sámi, experiencing rapid modernization, had adopted the majority population's ideals and even rejected their own Sáminess. One of the main reasons for this was the school system. After the war nearly the whole Sámi population became literate - but in a language foreign to them. On the other hand the contrasts they experienced caused them problems in relating to their own culture.

Due to long distances and wilderness conditions, children were sent to central schools, staying in boarding houses set up for that purpose, and going home on the weekends or, at the middle school level, only on long holidays and in summer. For instance, the trip from Vuovdaguoika in the Deatnu River valley to the Ivalo boarding house was 200 kilometres of bumpy, muddy, gravel roads in terrible condition, in the 50s and 60s. It was not possible to go home more than twice in a school year. Some children were only able to go home at Christmas and in summer. No wonder that "the distance between home and school widened the older one became", as writer Rauni-Magga Lukkari says in one of her poems.

Life in the boarding schools was hard. "Serving in an army barracks was more home-like than attending school and living in the boarding houses in Riutula and Anár", Sámi leader Oula Näkkäläjärvi stated. The usual troubles of normal youth were compounded for Sámi. Living in an environment of a foreign language and foreign opinions caused feelings of insecurity, stemming from being different and being harassed for it: intimidation was accompanied by shame for oneself and one´s background.

The time spent at the boarding houses also caused a break in the children's natural relationship with their home environment. Sámi languages were not read or heard in these institutions. Language and traditional skills transmitted throughout centuries - for example reindeer herding or handicrafts - were forgotten or never learned. In the schools and boarding houses children be-

came accustomed to the rules and customs of Finnish, Norwegian, Swedish, or Soviet Russian society. It affected everything from the way to dress to behaviour and even spiritual values.

Teacher Iisko Sara described the influence that the years of reconstruction had on Finnish Lapland, saying that in the end Sámi wanted to become more Finnish than the Finns themselves. They believed that in order to succeed they and their children would have to adopt the Finnish language and Finnish value system. In short - to change their identity. "Unfortunately, Sámi rarely succeeded, if ever", Sara said.

The situation on the Norwegian side of the border was the same. One wanted to secure for one's children the necessary willingness or readiness to adapt to Norwegian society, and that was seen possible only through being taught in the Norwegian language. Attempts by the school boards to make changes toward more Sámi content were met, above all, by opposition from the Sámi permanent residents. The Sámi position was naturally still influenced by the memory of the old Norwegianization policies.

In 1976, the Ninth Sámi Conference was held at the Anár elementary school, which was the school and boarding house environment for many young Sámi. Source: *Lapin kansa* archive.

THE AANAAR SÁMI – A MINORITY WITHIN A MINORITY

The Lake Aanaar Sámi (in their own language *sämmilaš*; in North Sámi *Anáráš*) are in many ways a rare group. Among the Sámi, they are one of the smallest minorities that has persisted. They number about 900, but the Aanaar language, which is truly a full-fledged language of its own, is spoken as a first language by only 350 people. It is also the only language group that lives within the borders of one country. "If the Aanaar Sámi disappear in Finland, they disappear from the whole world", declared the Aanaar Sámi leader Matti Morottaja.

Aanaar Sámi (Anár in North Sámi) represent the most traditional Sámi culture in Finland. Their language belongs to the Eastern Sámi language group, but clearly differs from the others. They have many traits in common, but the differences are even in the basic vocabulary. In North Sámi "fish" is *guolli*, in Aanaar it is *kyeli* and in Skolt *kue'll*. Respectively "mother" is *eadni, enni, jeä'n'n*. On the other hand, when we "pass by" in North Sámi it is *meattá*, in Aanaar *lappad* and in Skolt *rääi*. "Cat" is *bussá, kissá* and *kaass* in the respective languages.

Culturally they differ greatly from other Sámi groups. Aanaar Sámi were fishermen, who in the 1800s lived very isolated around the Great Lake, Lake Aanaar. Because of seasonal fishing at the Arctic Ocean their connections with Várjavuotna were close. This can be seen in the decorations of the Aanaar garment, which is reminiscent of the Várjjat dress; the same is true of certain language traits.

An identity without protection

Traditionally Aanaar Sámi were known for humility. Many historic sources record how little was needed to satisfy an Aanaar Sámi or keep them from despairing. In the 1600s the Aanaar Sámi were already recognized to adapt well even in matters of religion: they were "of all their forefathers and rejectors of faith the most pliant", as one of the ministers uttered.

Matti Morottaja characterized the time of those humble tribal people ironically, "Aanaar Sámi's too great compliance truly hastened their demise as a group. They did not stand up to defend their interests. Compared to the Ohcejohka Sámi, for example, who are irritable as lemmings, they are really peaceful folk... Authorities must be respected." One churchman taught that by giving liberal beatings with a broom handle.

The ability to adapt was needed later, as well. In the history of the Aanaar Sámi, the problems of a population spread thinly over a large area became ever greater. The Reindeer Sámi lived in touch with Aanaar Sámi for a long time, but after the borders were drawn by the end of the 1880s they settled in their area in great numbers.

The numbers of Finnish settlers also grew during that century. In 1800 they numbered about twenty, but before the end of the century they outnumbered the Aanaar Sámi. A third group was the Skolt Sámi, who were relocated after the war to the Lake Aanaar area. The adjustments of the three groups of people to the situation resulted in changes in reindeer herding, other livelihoods, and in their cultures.

The necessity to adapt is partly why the Aanaar Sámi identity was particularly susceptible in the 1900s. They did not have any particular symbols that they could hold fast to. Where Sámi are often widely characterized by reindeer herding and the tradition of yoik, the Aanaar Sámi did not know either of those.

With their early conversion to Christianity the old yoik tradition completely disappeared. In place of reindeer herding that was widespread among other Sámi, Aanaar Sámi had always based their livelihoods on a mixed economy. In addition to fishing they practised small scale reindeer keeping, small scale hay-dairy farming and activities of a seasonal nature, such as hay making and berry picking.

In the early stages many Sámi in Aanaar became colonists and their lifestyle began to change to the Finnish ways. For that reason, outsiders, except for ministers and linguists, often did not regard the Aanaar Sámi as a distinct group. In comparison, the semi-nomadic Skolt Sámi of Suo'nn'jel (Suonnjel) were studied with great interest, for example, by ethnologists. The same was true of the way government officials treated these groups.

A study of the legal history would need to be carried out in order to clarify the rights of descendants of members of the Aanaar siida to land and natural resources. A most important measure for securing their language would be to have an interpreter position in the Language Office of the Sámediggi in Finland.

Aanaar Sámi who have lived in the Lake Aanaar environment have been under pressure by many population groups. Photograph of Valpu Mattus by Jorma Puranen in Nellim (Njellim, Njeä'llem) in 1979.

Modern means

The group identity of Aanaar Sámi is founded on the coherence of families and kin groups. In comparison with other Sámi groups, it has been seen as a problem that Aanaar Sámi do not have a central village like Če'vetjäu'rr for the Skolt Sámi. There is also an old tradition: Aanaar Sámi lived in their areas all year round, unlike the Skolt Sámi whose many kin groups only came together in the winter village before they were relocated.

Preservation of their language is a prime means to preserve Aanaar Sámi identity. Work in that direction has been ongoing since the 1980s. In 1986 *Anaraškiela servi* (Aanaar Language Association) was founded. It is an association that tries to keep this issue alive in the public eye. It publishes the

magazine *Anaraš*, which carries easy-to-read articles of general interest as a way of encouraging greater use of the language. The association boasts one of the largest memberships among Sámi associations - around 180 members.

Sámi Radio has broadcast programs in the Aanaar Sámi language since the beginning of the 1980s. Main items are news, interviews, and music. The "Language Minute" presents questions regarding language maintenance and use. The greatest problem for the instruction of this language in schools has been the lack of teaching materials, especially past the primary level. The few teachers must still develop them themselves almost from nothing.

Aanaar Sámi has been taught several hours a week in the primary schools since the mid 1970s. During the 1996-1997 school year it was

taught in six primary schools in Aanaar municipality to 26 pupils and to four in the high school at Ivalo. The Aanaar Sámi "language day care", begun in 1997, tries to secure the language skills of children younger than school age, i. e. seven years. Adult education is organized through courses at the University of Oulu and at the Regional Sámi Education Centre in Aanaar.

In all such activities, it can be seen what is characteristic of minority groups in general: there are few knowledgeable and active people. As Matti Morottaja says, "The same person ends up being teacher, producer, cultural activist, lawyer, musician, artist, author, researcher, politician and youth promoter."

THE SKOLT SÁMI IN FINLAND

The Skolt Sámi (in their own language simply *sä'mmlaž* = a Sámi; in North Sámi *nuortalaš* = easterner) almost in their entirety had to abandon their original home region. The Njauddâm Skolt siida (*siid*) in far northeastern Norway no longer exists because nearly all members were assimilated into the Norwegian or Finnish culture.

After 1944, when Finland lost the Peäccam (Petsamo) District, the Skolt Sámi fled and were relocated in the vicinity of Lake Aanaar. On the Russian side the remaining Skolt Sámi were resettled and concentrated far from the border in the interior parts of the Kola Peninsula.

A troubled history

Some Skolt Sámi became part of Finland in the Tartu Peace Treaty signed between Finland and the Soviet Union in 1920. The border cut off the connections of western Skolt Sámi on the Finnish side from their more easterly relatives for 70 years. It split the Suo'nn'jel Skolt area so that one quarter remained on the Russian side. The siida lost a portion of its reindeer pastures and the traditional winter village.

The Finnish State built a new winter village for them in the 1930s consisting of some 20 log houses, a school with boarding facilities, and a frontier guard post. The language used in the school was Finnish, however.

The Suo'nn'jel (Suonnjel) area had a special status in that it was protected against expanding agricultural colonization and was planned to be an area for the protection of the Skolt Sámi culture;

Skolts had the exclusive right to fishing in the area's waters. The Second World War prevented the realization of that plan.

Instead, in other areas of Peäccam (Beahcán), Skolts were not given rights or protection. The Paaččjokk (Báhčaveadji) and Peäccam (Beahcán) Skolt areas were important for Finnish agricultural colonization and other sources of Finnish commerce and livelihood. The Forest Skolt siidas were especially vulnerable to changes because they needed the use of large areas. The loss of even one section of the area broke down the seasonal cycle of reindeer nomadism.

The Peäccam (Beahcán) Skolt migrations to the Arctic Ocean coast stopped as did ocean fishing in the 1920s and 1930s. Having given up their traditional ways of livelihood, the Skolt Sámi had a difficult time adapting to the values and customs of a new society. Matters were further worsened by the prejudices and nationalistic attitudes of the Finnish population. Finnish literature from Petsamo in the 1920s and 1930s is full of contemptuous and even racist images of Skolts.

World War II completely devastated the Skolts' lives. The Skolts were evacuated farther into Finland both during the Winter War and the Continuation War with the Soviet Union (November 1939 to September 1944). After the Lapland War with Germany (September 1944 to April 1945) the Skolts were gradually relocated into the Nellim-Lohttu region south of Lake Aanaar in the eastern part of Aanaar municipality.

The Skolt Sámi home or kinship areas were ceded, under the peace

treaty, to the Soviet Union. It was very clear that particularly the younger generations of the Skolts did not want to return there. After a four year process of planning, the Skolts who had formerly lived in Finnish Petsamo (Peäccam) area were relocated in areas north and south of Lake Aanaar in the fall of 1948: the Skolts from Suo'nn'jel (Suonnjel) were resettled in the Če'vetjäu'rr area, the others in the Nellim (Njellim, Njeä'llem) area.

In the new settlement areas, the Skolts were located on kinship groups, but the notable difference from their life in Peäccam was the cessation of their annual seasonal migrations. For example, in the narrow lake zone where the permanent homes of the Sue'nn'jel Skolts were located, there was no longer a summer area nor a winter village. There were great problems in reindeer herding since 4000 head of reindeer had been left on the Soviet Union side.

The Skolts' life changed drastically from what it had been previously in Peäccam (Beahcán). Their traditional livelihoods did not ensure a secure economic base. For instance, in the period between 1960 and the 1980s, reindeer herding as a primary source of income declined dramatically.

It became necessary to provide for the future and continuity of Skolt Sámi culture through special laws and measures. Despite that, the rate of unemployment was high, and nearly one quarter of the Skolt population moved away from the new settlements, especially to the capital of Finland, Helsinki.

It is estimated that there are around 500 Skolts. Their culture is distinctive in comparison to other Sámi cultures. Among other influences, Skolt culture received influences from the Russian Orthodox religion of the Karelian Russian culture. Cultural characteristics that differ from other Sámi are, for example, the Karelian style of folk dances and garments. The Skolt Sámi have a rare form of yoik, the *leudd*, a long poetic ballad style that persisted well under the domain of the tolerant Orthodox Church.

The old traditions of the Village Meeting have been preserved by the Skolt Sámi. In the ancient Skolt siida custom the Village Meeting makes decisions on issues of general concern. A 'person of trust' or headman with official authority is elected to administer these decisions. The problem for the Skolt Village Meeting is the same as for the modern Sámediggi - it does not have the power to decide over the use of their areas nor over property rights.

The dissimilarity of the Skolt Sámi culture from the cultures of Finns and other Sámi caused great problems during the postwar period. Outside of the Skolt area especially, the young Skolts suffered because of persistent negative attitudes. "If we wear our own traditional clothes we are seen as Gypsies or Russkies," a Skolt recounted to an interviewer. It was not only Finns, "other Sámi call us those names".

Sinikka Semenoja from Če'vetjäu'rr reports the burdensome legacy of the negative and discriminatory situation which the school environment left on the souls of the Skolt Sámi born in the 1950s and 1960s. Teachers turned a blind eye during the recess to violence which was strongly directly towards Skolt pupils. The most usual way to cope was to hide one's own background and even to completely deny it.

The orthodox religion clearly distinguished the Skolt Sámi from other Sámi groups in Finland. Ella Sarre in the Nellim (Njellim, Njeä'llem) *tsasouna* (chapel) in 1989. Photo: Kalle Kuittinen.

According to Semenoja, there is some light in the situation, "The positive approach to Sámi issues has reflected on Skolt lives as well. Skolt Sámi have official status in the Skolt area, literature has appeared in the Skolt language, and it is possible to visit the Kola Sámi. It is interesting that youth and children relate to their own Skolt Sámi background as a natural part of their identity. They want to learn Skolt Sámi, wear Sámi clothing, etc."

Če'vetjäu'rr is considered the centre of Skolt culture. A new school that included the upper level classes was built there in 1990. With the new school the instruction of Skolt Sámi increased, and even is taught as mother tongue. In general, however, Skolt Sámi is treated as a foreign language in Če'vetjäu'rr as well as in other schools in Municipality of Anár.

The problem is that few children and youth speak Skolt Sámi as their mother tongue. In 1993 the municipality implemented a Skolt Sámi day care as an experiment. Its goal was to strengthen children's language skills by offering a day care facility in their own language. Based on positive experiences, the project continued from 1997 when it received funding from the European Union.

The Orthodox religion has been a special solidifying factor in Skolt culture. The festivities celebrating the tradition of the Patron Saint Trifon have brought residents together. In August, a pilgrimage ceremony is held in Njauddâm (Njávdán) and in Če'vetjäu'rr where the main Christmas celebration is conducted as well. In February, ceremonies are held in Nellim (Njellim, Njeä'llem). The Church there has chosen to use the Skolt language. In 1983 the first prayer book in the Skolt language was published. In the church services it has been possible to increase the use of the Skolt language because the travelling parish minister and the cantor are Skolt Sámi.

THE KOLA SÁMI: A CENTURY OF HISTORY

The fate of the eastern Sámi (in the Kildin Sámi language simply *sam'lenč*) in the 1900s is the most tragic of all the Sámi. The groups living on the Kola Peninsula underwent the curses of conflicts and that area's industries. Their traditional settlement and land use areas had to be abandoned, as well as the largest part of their livelihoods and former way of life. Of the three Kola Sámi languages, the disappearance of two - Ahkkil and Ter Sámi - is considered by researchers to have been nearly inevitable. In their place the possibilities for Kildin Sámi have begun to improve.

In the 1920s, events in this northern part of the Soviet Union caused a complete change for the Kola Sámi population. The effective economic exploitation of the Murmansk District was disastrous for the Sámi of the region. The mining and other industrial activities in the Kola Peninsula are concentrated along the corridor from Kandalakša to Murmansk and between the lakes Avvir and Umbajávri in the area of the Gory Hibinskie Tundra.

With the completion of the Murmansk railway in 1916, settlement and exploitation were directed northward. In the 1930s large copper and nickel ore deposits were found in the central part of the Kola Peninsula and the Severonickel or Monžegorsk Mining Collective Combine was founded for their exploitation. Industrialization requires electricity, which was provided by harnessing the region's swift rivers. The Murmansk fishing industry began to be developed. Industrial activities need labour,

thus the population exploded. In ten years the population of Kola had increased from 20,000 to 150,000 in 1933.

The Kola Sámi traditional siida system collapsed in the decades after the Russian Revolution in 1917. The Sámi lands and waters were nationalized and taken over by the Soviet State; according to the law on property ownership all natural resources became the possessions of the State. Reindeer herding began to be collectivized, which happened slower here than elsewhere. As industrialization proceeded and the administrative management of the area developed in the 1940s, all Sámi households were concentrated in kolkhoz (collective) settlements.

In 1937 the persecution of "enemies of the people", begun under Stalin's leadership, was also directed toward Sámi. The Soviet State classified Sámi according to the number of reindeer they owned into classes of wealth: rich or kulak, average, and poor. Persecution measures were aimed especially at the kulaks, whom they began to imprison. Their adult children were also transferred to labour camps.

The authorities feigned that there was a Sámi nationalistic organization aiming at Sámi independence. People suspected of espionage and planning sabotage were sentenced to execution or to labour camp, and appeals were not allowed. At least 15 Sámi were shot as enemies of the people. In 1975 the Tribunal of the Northern Military District returned civic rights to many Sámi sentenced without reasons, but this decision was not made public.

The siida areas were finally lost in the forced relocation linked to collectivization under the Soviet regime. Sámi were concentrated in large settlements as early as the 1930s, and the Sámi of the western part of the Kola Peninsula had to move a second time when the hydro-electric power plants were built on the Tuloma River. The second wave of forced relocation came in the 1960s, when in the end the Sámi villages were moved elsewhere out of the way of the reservoirs and other construction. Because of the strategic position of the Kola Peninsula, its interior was set aside as a military area where no one could go. These relocations destroyed the Čalmny-Varre Sámi siida, where ancient rock paintings were found. In the same manner, people were removed from the Arsjohka siida on the coast. In recent times there have been attempts to resettle people there.

Through forced relocation, the State concentrated the population in larger settlements that were easier to manage and from where it was more efficient to provide communications, shops and health services. Sámi were located in Luja'vrr (Lujávri), where most of the Kola Sámi live today. It is not their own 'national district' (Russian *okrug*) in the Russian administrative system, since many other nationalities live there as well. Sámi make up one third of the population of Luja'vrr, or about 900 people.

The size of the Kola Sámi population, some 1800 people, has remained about the same, while Kola has become a centre with a population of one million. While the Sámi were one fifth of the

The Kola Sámi were separated from the rest of Sápmi for close to 70 years. Contacts began to be found again during the 1980s. The *Oijar* ensemble at the *Davvi Suvvá* Festival in Gárasavvon in 1993. Photo: Jorma Lehtola.

population in 1897, today they represent a minority of less than 0.2 percent among 26 other nationalities as identified in the Russian census.

The mixing of nationalities is also evident in reindeer herding. The work of herding the reindeer is done in the sovkhoz (collective farm) by brigades each made up of some ten workers. The brigades comprise all nationalities. The participation of the Komi people in reindeer herding is noticeably greater than by Sámi, although there is no large difference in their numbers. In the early 1990s, of 904 Sámi in Luja'vrr only 74 were reindeer herders. A large portion (61 percent) of Sámi work in so-called unskilled jobs or are unemployed. This has resulted in economic, social and personal problems. With the decrease in traditional livelihoods, the solidarity of families as well as of family members weakens.

When the Soviet Union collapsed, it became possible for Kola Sámi to meet their own relatives on the Finnish side and other Sámi groups in the Nordic countries.

In 1992 their association, *Guoládatnjárga Sámisearvi* or *Associacija Kolskih Saamov* (GSS/AKS) (Sámi Association of the Kola Peninsula) became a member of the Sámiraᵭᵭi. This association has around 300 members. Nevertheless, their problems are greater than for the Sámi in the Nordic Countries. Education in the Russian language has given the youth a feeling of inferiority.

Jelena Sergejeva quotes a man from Luja'vrr as saying, "for many generations, with their mother's milk, Sámi have inherited fear, lack of self-reliance, poor self-esteem and a feeling of insecurity. It cannot be expected that the Russian Sámi will become very quickly free of those things that have been forever a part of their heritage."

Because of those circumstances, the Sámi language was only used within the confines of the family and on the tundra as a language for work. In those reindeer brigades where there are older Sámi reindeer herders, the language used in herding may still be Sámi. Children and young people, however, have become used to speaking Russian. In the 1980s, the Kildin Sámi language began to be taught in Luja'vrr primary school, but only in the first three classes. The main problem is that it is impossible to find a native speaking teacher even in Luja'vrr. Sámi children learn Sámi as a foreign language. The relations with Skolt Sámi in Finland have led to promising cooperative projects.

Kildin Sámi as a written language was developed in the 1930s. It was an effort to further education among the 'small peoples of the North'. At the end of that decade the project was discarded. Since the 1950s the written language has once again begun to be enhanced. A number of primers, dictionaries and teaching materials, and recently two books of children's poetry have been published both in Kildin and North Sámi.

From Sámi renaissance to Álta

At the end of the 1960s, the Sámi movement began among young people, typically those of the first "boarding house generation". The background of the Sámi movement was the worldwide awakening of minorities defending their rights. Actually it was, however, a reaction against the postwar custom of trying to forget one's own cultural traditions and values by assimilating. It could only happen in a situation where the self esteem of a small people is threatened.

Peculiar to the movement at the turn of the 1970s was the breakthrough of Sámi culture into wide fronts, like at the beginning of the century: politics, media, culture and association activities. The arts were essential, above all literature and music, to spark the "Sámi Renaissance", as it is called (see sections on Sámi art).

Nils-Aslak Valkeapää raised the yoik to be the central symbol of national spirit, making it into a stage art through concerts, recordings, and publication. Music combined traditions and Sámi language with the influences from modern pop music. Writers committed themselves to building a new Sámi identity, sometimes tendentiously.

An important mark of the rise of the culture was the revival, in the beginning of the 1970s, of traditional handicrafts; the traditional *duodji* had to be taught to the young generation in many regions. The revival of traditional Sámi handicrafts resulted in their protection under *Sámi Duodji* trademark, specifically created for genuine Sámi work.

In Norway the central organization *Norgga Sámiid Riikkasearvi* (NSR) (Norway's National Organization of Sámi), founded in 1968, was a milestone among Sámi. Under its influence the attitudes of Norwegians began to change and the Sámi's concept of their own rights. The founding of the central organization initiated the birth of many local associations, such as in Romsa (Tromsa), Porsáŋgu and Deatnu in 1968, and in Bergen in 1969. During the 1970s, 13 Sámi associations came into being.

This central organization defined its goals to strengthen Sámi's position culturally, socially and economically. The most crucial fields were economic policies and the issue of Sámi rights. In its first meeting in Kárášjohka in 1969 NSR demanded the right of Sámi to decide on the use of natural resources in northern Norway. Since then land and water rights have been their most important themes. Later, during the Álta Conflict, the organization played a major role, and was later instrumental as the initiator for establishing the *Sámediggi* (Sámi Parliament) in Norway in 1989. It also dealt with the related question of voting of rights.

The most important political reforms took place in the early 1970s in Finland with the establishment of an elected Sámi representative body and in Norway with a scientific and educational institution.

In 1973, in an historic step, the Finnish Government created the Sámi Delegation (Finnish: *Saamelaisvaltuuskunta*), called by the Sámi *Sámi Parlameanta* (Sámi Parliament) by a statute proposed in the report of the State Committee for Sámi Affairs. By this statute, the Finnish Government officially recognized Sámi for the first time. The Sámi Delegation represented the official viewpoint of the Finnish Sámi. Later it became a model for the founding of the Sámediggi in Norway and Sweden.

In the early 1990s, the Delegation proposed changes to the legislation, and in 1995 the Law of Cultural Self-government was passed. It established the Sámediggi in Finland (Finnish: *Saamelaiskäräjät*), which replaced the Delegation and continued its work as the sole body that may represent the official Sámi viewpoint about issues concerning them.

In Norway relations with the Sámi minority from the 1970s onward were particularly laborious and it was impossible even to think of founding a Sámi representative body. However, the *Sámi Instituhtta* (Nordic Sámi Institute), a research and teaching centre, was founded in Guovdageaidnu in 1973. This was the fulfilment of a proposal made by the *Sámiráđđi* at the 1971 Jiellevárri Sámi Conference. Through this institute, the realms of education and science were given recognition and validity for the first time. The generally approved premise was that the institute should not have a local orientation, but should be a cooperative effort by all the Nordic countries. This has had a noticeable impact on the development of Sámi scientific endeavours and education, and also daily Sámi politics.

Sámi cooperation became active in three Nordic countries - Finland, Norway and Sweden - in the 1960s. The founding meeting of the *Johti Sabmelaččat* association in the spring of 1969. Photo: Kalle Kuittinen.

Leaders of two associations assembled together in 1971. One of the founders of *Samii Litto*, Nilla Outakoski (standing), discusses with Jouni Labba and Nils-Henrik Valkeapää of *Johti Sabmelaččat* Source: *Lapin kansa* archive.

The *Sámi Instituhtta* founded in 1973 got under its own roof in 1980. Observing the construction work are departmental head Samuli Aikio and the institute's first director Nils-Aslak Sara. Photo: Kalle Kuittinen.

The strength of the Sámi viewpoint is reflected in the institute's location in Guovdageaidnu in the heart of Sápmi, rather than in a university town like Romsa (Tromsa) or Ubmi, as had first been planned. The activism of young Sámi was specially instrumental in the final decision to locate their Sámi research centre in the middle of Sápmi and its daily life. The Institute's research activities and publications are studies on languages, history and culture, livelihood and legal history. Cooperative work with northern universities has been a very important part of its programme.

The Áltá Conflict

The basic premise of the Sámi's way of life has always been the gentle use of nature with long intervals to allow its recovery. Besides the physical adaptation, the connection to nature has marked the creation of communities with a framework in which they could make, in the best ways possible, suitable use of the limited production capacity of the subarctic environment. It is needless to exaggerate the Sámi's harmonious relationship to Nature, but it arose because the cycle of the renewable resource economy and its basis were not endangered.

Increased use of natural resources and direct exploitation due to the States' requirements for reconstruction after World War II unavoidably imperiled the Sámi way of life, and generated a growing counterreaction as well. The major cause of damage to the natural environment was the building of large dams, which began on some rivers as early as the 1930s. On the Norwegian side, about 60 river systems had been harnessed to provide electricity by the 1970s. On the Swedish side, the State's Vattenfall company dammed water systems, flooding large areas, destroying reindeer pastures needed for herding and wiping out the vital necessities for earning a living for the Forest Sámi as well. In the Kola region, environmental catastrophes affected everyone who depended on nature for a livelihood.

On the Finnish side, the most devastating environmental disturbance was the Lokka-Porttipahta dam planned in the 1950s and events connected with it. Environmental destruction, tourist facili-

ties and rapid technological development were especially fateful for the life of the reindeer herding Sámi of Soabbat. Their combined effects contributed to the disintegration of the foundation of Sámi culture.

On the Swedish and Norwegian sides, demonstrations against the dam constructions began in the 1960s. The largest and most well-known demonstration was the ten year conflict over the protection of the Áltá-Guovdageaidnu River system, lasting from 1968 to 1982. For the Sámi, the immediate issue was the right to decide on the use of their own areas.

The wider issue was concerned with observing the principles of the rule of law. The Sámi referred to the border treaty of 1751 in which Norway and Sweden-Finland guaranteed Sámi rights in their areas. In the Sámi view, these ownership rights could not legally be revoked anywhere in Sápmi.

The Sámi demanded recognition as an aboriginal people in the Norwegian Constitution, and that their economic and social foundations be protected. At the same time, they called for the establishment of a democratically elected Sámi political body. Sámi rights to land and water were to be clarified. Sámi language and culture should also be given official status. Before the events at Áltá, the official quarters turned a deaf ear to such demands; Norway's policies toward Sámi had always been the most severe of all the three Nordic states with Sámi populations.

The Norwegian State's position toward the demonstrators was uncompromising. They cleared the demonstrators' camps in January 1981. Work on the dam continued and the new power plant opened in 1987. Despite setbacks, the Áltá Conflict had striking consequences. The violence used by officials against the aboriginal population opened the eyes of many people - especially young people - and awakened the Sámi identity of many.

Particularly significant was the awakening of the self-esteem of the Sea Sámi, who until that time had been known as the most Norwegianized of all the Sámi groups. The Áltá Conflict had a great influence on Sámi art, because many artists participated in the struggle or had their "cultural awakening" through that experience. (See section on art). During the struggle the Sámi movement created a Sámi national symbol - the blue, red and yellow Sámi flag was raised defiantly on a pole in Stilla. The official design, differing slightly, was adopted in 1986.

The Áltá Conflict was remarkable politically because it caused Norway to change its official policy toward Sámi. After the conflict the State had to act. Its reputation in minority affairs had received a heavy blow, and there was no choice other than to take even the needs of Sámi into consideration in legislation. In 1980, the Norwegian government appointed a state committee on Sámi affairs to consider cultural and legal issues.

Within one decade of the Áltá Conflict, Sámi politics accomplished a large part of the reforms that the Sámi had demanded during that struggle. The Sámi were recognized as an aboriginal people under the amended Norwegian Constitution in 1988; obtained their own representative body, the Sámediggi, in 1989; received their own political advisory authority to the government, the Coordinating Committee on Sámi Affairs; and secured the Sámi language act in 1990.

The Sámi have also had to suffer environmental catastrophes which they had no possible way of influencing. The worst setback - in addition to the pollution problems in the Kola Peninsula - was the Chernobyl nuclear disaster in the spring of 1986. The pollution that came from the fires of the nuclear reactor in the Ukraine travelled on the wind to central Scandinavia, above all to the southern part of Sápmi in Sweden, the area of the South Sámi, where it came down in rain. The radio-active pollution binds especially in lichens, on which reindeer feed.

The cesium content of reindeer meat rose so high that it was unsafe for human consumption. In the Swedish Sámi area, reindeer were driven to mass slaughter that same fall. It is estimated that 30,000 head were slaughtered and buried. The problems of selling reindeer meat increased. Slaughtering began to take place in early fall before the animals started eating lichens. Complete renewal of the lichen cover is estimated to take 30 years. The Chernobyl catastrophe showed the vulnerability of a people following a nature based economy.

During the height of the Álta Conflict Gro Harlem Brundtland became Norway's prime minister.

In January 1981 the Norwegian government cleared the Stilla protest camp with police forces.

Sámi protesters also built a camp in front of the Storting in Oslo.

Artist Synnøve Persen (second from left) was part of the protest.

"Norway's laws? The Rights of the Sámi!" - Slogan and victory sign in front of the Storting in Oslo.

Niillas A. Somby maimed in his unsuccessful bridge explosion took his severed hand for propaganda usage. Together with Harry Johansen he photographed it placed on top of the Norwegian legal code book. This became the most famous photograph of the Álta Conflict. Photos on these pages: Niillas A. Somby.

THE ALTÁ CHRONICLE

In mid January 1981, in the bitter cold of mid-winter, the Áltá Conflict culminated in a police operation. The Norwegian government, in its determination to dam the Áltá River for energy production, took to violence against the Sámi demonstrators. Despite the defeat of the Sámi, the event marked a surprising turning point for Sámi in Norway, legally as well as culturally. It changed the State's position on Sámi, which until then had been characterized by a policy of Norwegianization.

The conflict over the construction on the Áltá-Guovdageaidnu watershed had begun more than ten years earlier. In 1968 the Norwegian state energy company NVE made a proposal for the regulation of the water system. The plan took in a large area, and included flooding the Sámi village of Máze by an artificial lake. The opposition movement begun in Máze ended in 1973 with a decision by the Norwegian Storting to spare that Sámi village. In 1976 a group of young Sámi artists gathered to work in Máze. Many of them became active in the Sámi national movement.

Disregarding the opposition of the local municipal governments of Guovdageaidnu and Áltá, the construction plans were revised and went ahead. In 1978 the Storting's proposal and decision to build the dam gave birth to a popular movement that quickly gathered supporters for its organization from neighbouring countries. In July 1979, demonstrators gathered at Stilla where the roadwork for the dam project had reached. Together with a demonstration held in Oslo,

they succeeded in stopping the roadwork.

The movement had two main focal points: the nature protection issue, whose leader was the Norwegian Alfred Nilsen; and the Sámi movement led by the central associations, the *Norgga Boazosápmelaččaid Riikkasearvi* (NBR: Sámi Reindeer Herders' Association of Norway) and the *Norgga Sámiid Riikkasearvi* (NSR: Norway's National Organization of Sámi). The nature protectionists opposed the construction on the basis of the ravages it would inflict on nature, as well as the damage it would cause to the livelihoods of the region. The Sámi fought for the future of reindeer herding and greater rights to govern in their own areas.

The Sámi front was by no means united. In 1979 Sámi who were loyal to Norway founded the new association, *Sámiid Ædnansærvi* (SLF or Samenes Landsførbund, Norwegian Sámi Union) to counter the NSR. Their goals were basically opposite. She SLF's statutes declared its intent to work for Norway's constitutional principles, respecting the King and his government. It opposed the NSR's "aggressive" policies and organized, among other things, a demonstration in support of damming the Áltá River.

The decision, made in September 1980, to continue building the road prompted the demonstrators to set up a permanent camp in Stilla. They refused to leave the area, chaining themselves together to prevent the bulldozers from working. In December 1980, Áltá's county assembly approved, by a narrow

margin, the State's intervention in the conflict. In the new year more than 600 police were sent to Áltá from southern Norway. The order was given by Prime Minister Oddvar Nordli. In mid January 1981 the police cleared the camp at Stilla.

Artist Ingunn Utsi was there and remembered later looking around her and thinking, "This is like war - against your own people." Nearly 500 demonstrators were fined. The expense of the police operations reached 60 million Norwegian crowns.

The means used in the conflict were questioned all the time. After the decision to go ahead with the construction, officials received warnings that there may even be suicide burnings; however, the proceedings were peaceful and without violence. In speeches and writings, the coming of the police by boat up the Áltá Fjord was compared to the arrival of German troops during World War II; the battleships had even anchored at the same place in spring 1940.

Many were reminded of the events in Guovdageaidnu in 1852 when Norwegian authorities heavy-handedly suppressed the Sámi "people's uprising". However, Sámi wanted to progress beyond the violence of the Guovdageaidnu Uprising.

After the forced removal of people from Stilla at the end of January 1981, ten Sámi - among them the artist Synnøve Persen - went on a hunger strike in front of the main entrance to the Storting building in Oslo. In the beginning of February, a new Prime Minister took office; Gro Harlem Brundtland and her new cabinet announced the

"Mi várjalit Sámi" (We will protect Sápmi, our land). After the clearing of the Stilla camp the protest continued in Oslo. The Sámi hunger strike stopped the Áltá road construction for some time. Photo: Niillas A. Somby.

stopping of the road construction until further notice. The government stressed that the decision was not due to pressure, but to the law on cultural artifacts, which required an inventory to be made of the archaeology in the area where the roadwork was to be carried out. The Sámi stopped their hunger strike, which had lasted more than a month. In September work on the road began again.

In March 1982 the situation took a dramatic turn. Two Sámi tried to blow up a bridge on the part of the road that had already been built. The photographer Niillas A. Somby lost a hand when he pressed the detonator too soon. Sámi reaction to this act of defiance was conflicting. For example, Aslak Nils Sara, the Sámi member of the World Council of Indigenous Peoples (WCIP), dissociated himself completely from it. Others felt it was justified.

Somby's history continued to be colourful. When he was freed from the prison in Romsa (Tromsa) for a court appearance, he unexpectedly fled via Finland to Canada. There he was not granted political asylum officially; he was adopted by an Indian band for his protection and concealment. Later Somby returned to Norway to finish his prison sentence.

In 1987 the new power station began producing electricity. Because of the opposition, the amount of power production was reduced and the structure was built in the cleanest possible way, taking into consideration the salmon spawning grounds. The effects of the power plant and dam have not been studied in depth. In 1990, just before her reelection as Norway's Prime Minister, Gro Harlem Brundtland admitted that the construction of the Áltá dam had been needless. The electricity it had produced had not had much economic significance.

77

Sámi politics straddling national borders

Sámi political activities were instrumental in the founding of the many local associations that arose in Norway, Sweden and Finland in the 1960s. However, a sense of community among the Nordic countries was the inspiration behind the idea of a Sámi community. The national borders created in the northern areas in the 1800s were a new phenomenon with a detrimental impact on Sámi culture, but they did not stop activities. In the Proceedings of the Jiellevárri Sámi Conference of 1971, an idea surfaced that sparked the interest of Sámi youth:

"We are one people. We have a common language, a common history and culture, and we have a strong feeling of belonging together. [..] We need to put in place in society our values, our cultures and ways of life and to have them accepted as valuable and as values to be developed. [..] We are Sámi and wish to be Sámi, we are not more nor less than other peoples."

The central voice of the society straddling the borders were the well-known, regularly held Sámi Conferences. According to Matti Morottaja they were "of course, only discussion forums, and their public impact did not have a great impact on the governments' direction, but they had a direct significance for raising a Sámi spirit of community." In the Conferences, questions on such themes as Sámi rights, livelihoods and culture were examined.

For example, at the 1971 Conference the proposal was made to establish a Nordic Sámi Institute, which became a reality two years later. At the 1976 Conference, the delegates decided to join the World Council of Indigenous Peoples (WCIP), reflecting the Sámi's previous efforts at cooperation with other peoples struggling with similar problems; the second meeting of the WCIP was hosted by Sámi and held in Kiruna in Sweden in 1977. In Helsinki in 1992 the 15th Sámi Conference made an historical decision designating the Sámi national day and other commemorative days.

Many of today's Sámi organizations unite Sámi from Sweden, Norway and Finland, and lately also include Sámi from Russia. Sámi teachers (1982), youth (1983) and Sámi women (1988) founded joint associations including the three or the four countries. The same has been done by representatives of different fields of art: writers (*Sámi Girječálliid Searvi*, 1979), visual artists (*Sámi Dáiddačehpiid Searvi*, 1979), musicians (*Sámi Musihkkariid Searvi*, 1982) and actors and theatre people (*Sámi Teáhtersearvi*, 1980). The creation of many organizations drew attention from the late 1960s into the 1990s. The sports association *Sámi Valaštallan Lihttu* was founded in 1969.

Another very visible indication of the cooperation of Sámi in the three Nordic countries is their shared trademark to protect items and handicrafts that are of genuine Sámi origin. In 1982 *Sápmelaš Duoddjarat r.y.* in Finland, *Sámiid Duodji* in Norway, and *Same-Ätnam* in Sweden agreed on the use of the trademark and it was sanctioned by Sámiraddi. The copyright and the rights to the use of the *Sámi Duodji* trademark belong to the Sámi artisans who have training and experience and are members of the aforementioned organizations. It tells the buyer that the maker of the item is a Sámi artisan and the work genuine.

The role of young people has been pivotal from the beginning. The youth organizations like *Teänupakti* on the Finnish side in the 1960s, and the *Kárášjohka Nuorai Sami Sær'vi* (1972) have organized youth camps, evening events, and took care of issues concerning young Sámi at the municipal level. The activities expanded across the borders in 1983 when the Sámi youth organization, *Sámi Álbmoga Nuoraid Searvi* (SÁNS) was founded. Right from the beginning they announced that they did not accept the national borders running through Sápmi.

Since the 1990s, SÁNS and all the new youth associations in the four countries, - *Suoma Sámi Nuorat* (SSN, 1991) in Finland, *Sáminuorra* in Sweden, *Davvi Nuorra* in Norway and *Saam Nuurš* in Russia - have organized camps and courses, and fostered connections to universities. Central issues were and are the self esteem and identity of young Sámi. For example, in 1996 the youth organized a demonstration in Rovaniemi, Finland, against using Sámi traditional garments for purposes of tourism.

The Sámiraŧŧi has been the unifying organization for the Sámi from three Nordic countries - and since 1992 also from Russia. At the meeting in 1994 the members discuss the foundation of an academy for Sámi art in Kárášjohka. Photo: Jaakko Alatalo.

The Sámi women's association *Sáráhkká - Sámi Nissonorganisašuvdna* (1988) was the first association in which Kola Sámi were fully integrated. The beginning was fairly dramatic. The Kola Sámi women, as citizens of the USSR, could not receive visas to attend the first annual meeting in Kárášjohka, Norway. Therefore, the event took place on the border bridge between Norway and Finland, and took on a symbolic significance.

Sáráhkká raised new questions in Sámi politics. The place of women in Sámi society was not as straightforward and equal as it may seem from the outside; the association drew serious attention to violence in the home, for example. It pressured for the securing of women's legal status. It also was concerned with child raising. *Sáráhkká* had a significant role in the founding of the *International Indigenous Women's Council* (IIWC).

With the advent of Perestroika at the end of the 1980s, the Kola Sámi joined the general Sámi activities. The *Guoládatnjárga Sámisearvi / Associacija Kolskih Saamov* (Sámi Association of the Kola Peninsula) was founded in 1989 to represent the affairs of the two thousand Sámi on the industrial and strategic peninsula. The Russian Sámi became members of Sámiraŧŧi in 1992. The 1996 Sámi Conference was held in Murmansk, Russia.

From the beginning, Sámi have been active in indigenous peoples affairs. There are more than 300 million indigenous people (*álgoálbmogat* in Sámi) in 70 countries. Cooperation among indigenous peoples was sparked by their similar histories and common experiences. At the First Arctic People's Conference held in Copenhagen in 1973, representatives of North American Indians, Inuit, Kalaallimiut (Greenlanders) and Sámi met.

The conference appointed a working group, who drafted a proposal for creating the *World Council* of *Indigenous Peoples*, which was founded two years later in 1975. North, Central and South American aboriginal peoples sent large delegations to the founding meeting. The Maori of New Zealand were well represented at that meeting, as were the Kalaallimiut of Greenland and the Sámi. Australian aboriginals and Hawaiians also sent their own representatives. The WCIP organizes general meetings every three to four years.

From the beginning, the Council has emphasized two issues: indigenous rights to ownership of land and water, and the right to self-determination. The impact of Sámi membership in the WCIP, as well as their visibility in UN activities, has been felt in Nordic politics as well. Sámi issues have risen in the society regionally, and are no longer marginal questions, but have become questions that have an important significance for the national governments' abilities to function in an international capacity.

Sámi administration today

Today Sámi in Sweden, Norway and Finland each have their own representative body - Sámediggi (Sámi Parliament). Finnish Sámi were the pioneers, founding the *Sámi Parlameanta* in 1973. Its mandate was to "oversee Sámi rights and promote Sámi economic, social and cultural well-being".

In 1995 the Law on Cultural Self-government was passed in Finland. It strengthened the position of the Sámediggi by creating even greater possibilities for Sámi to participate in preparing solutions on issues concerning them. Under this law the elected president occupies a permanent full-time salaried position. The Sámediggi also has the power to decide on the distribution of finances to support cultural programs, which had previously been decided by the Finnish ministry of education. These funds are earmarked for Sámi culture in general and for development of teaching materials. In 2002, social and health services were added to the Sámediggi's responsibilities.

The Sámediggi has 21 members, at least three from each municipality in the Finnish part of Sápmi. They are elected every fourth year. The assembly has five committees that make presentations on issues from economic policy to cultural

concerns. The secretariat, located in Anár, Finland, has a general office; an office of education and for educational materials; and an office of Sámi languages which is charged, above all, with the implementation of the language law. There are nine permanent employees.

Eligible to vote are all Sámi who are on the Sámediggi's approved voter list, taken from the Sámi Registry. According to the statutes, a Sámi is a person who feels oneself to be Sámi, and "who learned Sámi as whose first language, or at least one of whose parents or grandparents learned Sámi as their first language". In 1996 the additional definitions were drafted to the law on cultural self-government, which would have widened the language restrictions to include outsiders. Because of difficulties arising from such an expansion, it was advised to leave the definition unchanged, thus based on language.

The Sámi Parliament of 1973 on the Finnish side established a model which became the basis for the Norwegian (1989) and Swedish (1993) Sámi Parliaments. The definition of Sámi is the same in those countries. For instance, the Norwegian Sámediggi's Sámi registry lists any person who feels oneself as Sámi, and who either knows the Sámi language or at least one of whose parents or grandparents spoke Sámi as their mother tongue. In Russia the official definition of a Sámi is different. At 16 years of age a person may announce the "nationality" to which they wish to belong. This happens in connection with the issuing of passports. Sámi "nationality" is listed in the passport.

In Norway the Sámediggi was formed and began functioning in 1989. This had been one of the most important demands in the Álta Conflict, the Sámi's own representative body that makes statements on issues affecting Sámi. The difference between the Finnish Sámediggi and the Norwegian Sámediggi is that, from the beginning, the Norwegian body was able to have a greater influence. Right from the start its first president, Ole Henrik Magga, a professor of linguistics, filled the office with great competence and raised the Sámediggi's profile and authority.

The Norwegian Sámediggi has accomplished a great deal. It has noticeably influenced the situation of the Sea Sámi and issued creative propos-

Cooperation with other aboriginal peoples has been fruitful for Sámi, because many problems are the same. An initiator of this cooperation was Nils-Aslak Valkeapää. This drawing from his *Ruoktu váimmus* collection was influenced by his travels to American Indians among whom «appeared a sister, a brother was found».

als on issues of land ownership. Special was, for example, that they wanted to divide the water rights for sea fishing into areas rather than according to ethnic boundaries. This increased trust in the Sámediggi among non-Sámi as well. Land ownership also was considered on the basis of area.

Sceptical voices were also heard, of course. Some Sámi asked whether the Sámediggi had actual powers or whether it had been founded only to assuage the conscience of Norwegian politicians. They emphasized that the Sámediggi should have decision-making powers in matters concerning Sámi, the present advisory capacity is available to every citizen.

The Sámediggi received credibility from the unexpected bold support of the King of Norway. From the very beginning, King Olaf and his successor King Harald opened the sessions of the Sámediggi. Thus, as far as the King's involvement is concerned, the Sámediggi is comparable to the Norwegian Storting. At the 1997 opening session, King Harald held a radical political speech on Sámi rights and apologized for the past actions of the Norwegian government toward the Sámi.

The Swedish Sámediggi has 31 members, who are elected to four year terms. The Sámediggi distributes funds from State financial support and from the Sámi Foundation to promote Sámi culture and organizations. It appoints the board of directors for Sámi schools, directs work connected with Sámi language, cooperates with community projects, represents reindeer herding interests, and reports on Sámi conditions. The Sámediggi in Sweden does not have the power to decide on certain issues, for instance, on land use.

In Finland, the Sámediggi has had similar problems. One of the main difficulties is the lack of decision making powers; the States are not yet ready to grant ownership rights to Sámi in their own areas. One example is the practical problem drawing up the Sámi registry. In 1993 the number of registered Sámi voters was only 7300 in Norway and 5300 in Sweden, although the actual number of Sámi is many times greater.

On the Finnish side the present number, around 7000, is nearly correct, because the registration has been carried out for a longer time, beginning

with the State committee report census of 1952. Attention has also been given to the under-representation of women in the Sámediggi. In 1997 the Norwegian Sámediggi had 39 members, 10 were women. In Finland there are only four women out of 21 members.

The Norwegian government had a Sámi political advisor to the Ministry of Local Government, which was changed to a national secretariat in 1997. The Swedish state council began working with an advisor for Sámi affairs, the Sámi ombudsman, in 1962. The office mainly clarified issues relating to the Sámi legal situation. In the Swedish government a ministry is also responsible for Sámi affairs; it has been the Ministry of Agriculture.

The Finnish government or Parliament have not created similar positions for experts on Sámi affairs. In Finland the Sámi Affairs Committee, created in 1960, functions in a different manner, working in cooperation with the Ministry of Justice to draft joint proposals on issues that affect Sámi.

The Skolt Sámi have the Skolt Sámi Village Meeting, their own traditional governmental model based on the old self-governing siida system. Among the Skolt Sámi, the siida system was maintained until 1944, when the Skolts had to leave their home areas in the Soviet Union. Although they left their previous way of life of a yearly cycle, they kept alive the tradition of the village meeting. The person of trust, or headman, functions as the official Skolt representative, who simultaneously is employed part-time in the Sámi Affairs Committee. The village meetings make official proposals and position statements on issues concerning Skolt Sámi.

The Sámiráđđi continues to be the organ for cooperation among Sámi and Sámi organizations in the four different countries. It plays an important role as the unifying body for the Sámi national organizations, and tries to look after Sámi interests internationally. The Sámiráđđi was instrumental in bringing about the Joint Parliamentary Council of the Sámi Parliaments, for which the agreement was signed at Romsa (Tromsa) in February 1997 to commemorate 80 years of Sámi cooperation.

The work of the Sámiráđđi directs and oversees

In Finland the Sámediggi, which began its work in 1996, continued the tasks of the Sámi Delegation. It has received plenty of additional independence. Pekka Aikio began as its first chair or president; he was already the secretary of the committee that proposed the first delegation founded in 1973. Photo: Jorma Lehtola.

At the opening of the Sámediggi in Ohcejohka in March 1996, professors Pekka Sammallahti (left) and Ole-Henrik Magga, who was the president of the Sámediggi in Norway until 1997, sit next to Pekka Aikio. Photo: Satu Natunen.

Sámi cooperation across borders has been natural, although the state boundaries have interfered with it. Kalle Mannela, reporter with Sámi Radio, enjoys the company of eastern Sámi. Photo: Jorma Lehtola.

83

the Sámi Conferences, which are organized in a different part of Sápmi every fourth year. It is a true international aboriginal body and functions as an independent Non-Governmental Organization (NGO) in the United Nations. It is also an active participant in the World Council of Indigenous Peoples (WCIP) and the Arctic Council.

The Sámiráđđi has 15 members appointed by the Sámi Conference: four from Finland, four from Sweden, five from Norway, and two from Russia. It meets twice a year. The Council's secretariat is located in Ohcejohka in Finland. In 1998 the Council was restructured to include Sámi from Russia. Delegates to the Sámi Conference are nominated by member organizations of the Sámiráđđi. There are in all 65 delegates, 20 each from Finland, Sweden, and Norway, and five from Russia, corresponding to the size of the Sámi population in each country.

Sámi rights

The Sámi's work in the World Council of Indigenous Peoples follows the same direction that has been the central issue in Sámi politics since the 1960s. Sámi have claimed rights to land, water and traditional livelihoods which the Nordic countries do not acknowledge. They quote the age-old usage (usufruct), the traditional property rights of the Sámi siidas, which were officially recognized by the authorities in earlier times. Officially these rights were written down most prominently in the Strömstad Border Treaty between Sweden and Denmark-Norway in 1751, which strengthened the special position of Sámi. According to the Sámi, during the course of the 1800s and 1900s, the States began, without any knowledge of the legal basis, to set boundaries to the lands and waters belonging to the Sámi siidas.

The conflict over ownership rights has often been a side issue. The *Skattefjällmålet* (The Tax Mountain Case) was a 15 year legal struggle of the Sámi in Jämtland Province in Sweden against the Swedish State. They tried to prove their ownership of certain mountain areas on the basis of usage since time immemorial. In 1981 - the year of the Álta Conflict - the Supreme Court of Swe-

den handed down the decision that the State owned the disputed areas. Still, the court found that Sámi had strong usufruct rights in the area, based on age-old usage.

On the Finnish side, the Sámi political view on ownership culminated in the 1970s when, based on the Land Reform Law, surveys began to define borders for water districts, thus dividing the lands and waters in the northern parts of the Province of Lapland. Based on the property allotment, farmsteads were established, which had rights to a certain size of water areas. The Sámi felt that the border surveys were illegal because they split the water areas belonging to the siida. In their opinion, the issue was a larger political question: now it was not only the water areas that were divided, but land as well. The Sámi proved the question of land ownership had not been clarified. The results of the research on legal history begun by the Sámi Institute were already put to use with respect to the question of property ownership.

Research on Sámi rights has been a central activity of the Sámi Institute. It began in 1973 as a project that was to use historical research methods as a basis to obtain a picture of Sámi rights to lands and waters in their own areas. The most notable result has been the work by Kaisa Korpijaakko, *Sámi Legal Status in Sweden-Finland*, published in 1989, which documents in detail Sámi land ownership in the 1700s. In her most recent research, released in 1999, Korpijaakko attempts to show under which circumstances Sámi rights were reversed in the usage by officials.

Sámi considered the conflict over the Álta River as an actual struggle for their rights to lands and waters. In Norway a significant achievement was the establishment, in the aftermath of the Álta Conflict, of the Committee on Sámi Rights. The recognition of Sámi rights in the constitution of 1988, the founding of the Sámediggi, and the Sámi Language Act were in part the results of the extensive research by this committee to settle Sámi rights.

In 1990 Norway ratified the International Convention on Indigenous Populations (No. 169) of the International Labour Organization (ILO). According to it, Sámi are recognized as an aboriginal people, not merely an ethnic minority, such as, for example, immigrants and refugees. The ILO convention requires and exhorts mutual respect and equality presupposing the commensurate and just treatment of aboriginal peoples in preserving their language and culture. In other words, special means should be used, for example, in settling property rights questions.

Sweden, Finland and Russia have not yet ratified the ILO convention. A problem for those countries is the obligation to recognize the aboriginal peoples' property rights with certain conditions. In Finland and Sweden, Sámi rights as an aboriginal people do not comply in every part of their implementation to the international human rights convention.

Finland was in the first group of states that ratified the preliminary agreement on minority rights in 1995. In doing so, Finland agreed to much tighter commitment than Norway, for example, to secure the status of Sámi languages through special measures.

In Sweden, as in Finland, there has long been talk of a Sámi Law that would possibly transfer "state lands" to Sámi administration. As an example, in Finland in 1952, 1973 and 1990, State committees proposed a law to settle land and water rights. A sensitive issue is who ultimately owns the lands in Sápmi presently controlled by the Parks and Forestry Service. The responsible ministry or board has never addressed the issue of land rights.

Also the Sámi in Sweden have on several occasions expressed disappointment that a Sámi Law has not been realized and that the government has not ratified the ILO convention on aboriginal peoples. A Sámi Law would give Sámi the right to control their own lands and waters. In the present circumstance, the State sees itself as the land owner in the North. The Sámi have emphasized that the most important issue is not ownership per se, but the right to use the lands and waters in accordance with their own wishes.

The demands for a Sámi Law have caused conflicts between Sámi and residents who moved into local communities as colonists. For example, in 1998 the Swedish property owners in Härjedal, Sweden began a court case against Sámi over usage rights to areas of reindeer pastures.

On the Finnish side, the controversy created over legality of Sámi land rights has sparked Finnish land owners' fear that State lands may be transferred to Sámi control. That fear has stirred up claims that changes in ownership rights would lead to Finns being expelled from Lapland. In northern Norway, there has been a "No to Sámiland" movement, which has sparked a Sámi counter movement.

Right to one´s own language

The Sámi have emphasized in their language policy that they are not a language minority, but rather an aboriginal people, having their own language and culture. For that reason the governments have a greater responsibility for Sámi language rights than they have for such minorities whose language preservation is based on the situation in their mother country. There is no country to offer protection for the language and culture of the Sámi, such as many other minorities have.

The importance of the mother tongue for a child's emotional development has been understood for a long time. The position of the church, and later of the school, which they each sporadically carried out, was the idea that only through instruction in the mother tongue is it possible to internalize understanding and feelings. Through their first language, or mother tongue, children receive a foundation in their emotional life and develop self-confidence. The second learned language may remain only on the level of rational thought.

An individual assimilates the world as feelings and images that are bound in their own language. Author Kerttu Vuolab states that "only in the Sámi language do I have the taste of life. I experienced it through living and feeling. Later I learned the Finnish language in school and in books. It was something I learned from the outside. A foreign language is always a limited tool, it doesn't have the depth of life."

TRANSFORMING IDENTITIES

Oslo, Stockholm and Helsinki are playfully referred to be the largest Sámi villages or siidas in the Nordic countries. Some 5000 Sámi live in Oslo. These Sámi, for different reasons, left their home communities to work, study, or do something else. Some have settled permanently in the capital city.

Around 1800 Sámi are registered as living outside Sápmi in Finland. Some 500 live in Helsinki. In the Rovaniemi region there are some 250 permanent Sámi residents and around one hundred students. There is also a noticeable Skolt Sámi minority of about 50 people. The Sámi association *Mii* (We) organizes evening programmes and larger events, such as the Skolt Sámi cultural festival in 1996.

The urban Sámi communities are a good example of the evolving Sámi identity that is brought about by new times. It is for many - outsiders as well as Sámi themselves - a puzzling and confusing matter.

Migrating identities

Questions of ethnicity and identity arose particularly in the 1900s becoming important in the discussion concerning Sámi as a separate people. What actually is a *Sámi*?

In the old way of thinking, a "Lapp is a Lapp" when she/he lives in a sod hut or tent. The police chief in Ohcejohka in the 1930s, E. N. Manninen, said of his Sámi friend, "he is not a real 'Lapp' because he eats with a knife and fork".

Nowadays a "real" Sámi may be a city dweller, may be a professional computer programmer, or an astronomer. Theoretically, the question is the idea of an evolving identity. In the conventional view an individual's identity is a complete and unchanging "being", an essence that is preserved in the traditional knowledge of the individual and of the people. "Genuine" knowledge requires weeding out everything foreign or at least confining it clearly to the outside.

In the modern view identity is an on-going process, continually being produced. There is no such thing as a complete and unchanging identity; it is in certain ways created all the time. It changes through time and history. Identities are changeable or, better said, migrating (*johtti*) as Sámi researcher Rauna Kuokkanen defines.

The changes in Sámi culture emerging in the 1960s and 1970s illustrate this development. As times changed Sámi have had to let go many traditional models, nevertheless taking on new forms adapted to the new circumstances. The idea of "genuine Lapp" would have led to cultural atrophy. Consciousness of their own culture's life force has made it possible to assimilate new influences without prejudice. In turn, this has led to the rise in the culture's esteem.

A common difference

Because identities are dynamic in flux, they are difficult to define. What is the measure of Sámi identity? The characteristics of an ethnic group have to be identified theoretically. In 1965 the Finnish sociologist Erkki Asp examined Sámi identity by including criteria such as reindeer driving, staying over night in sod huts and using reindeer milk. Traditionally, being Sámi was considered to be connected to reindeer herding, language and traditional livelihoods in Sápmi.

For the younger generations of Sámi, those criteria are no use as identifying features. A person should not "have" to speak Sámi in order to be a Sámi. Someone who is on the voter list of the Sámediggi does not necessarily have to live in Sápmi. On the other hand, a person who is a reindeer herder is not a Sámi unless she or he also has other characteristics that mean being a Sámi. The problem of defining Sámi identity was brought to the fore during the so-called "conflict over Lappishness" which arose in Finland over the Law on Cultural Self-government, passed in 1995. Under its new, wider definition of Sámi, some people who were not recognized by the Sámediggi tried to register as Sámi.

The problem stemmed from the law's allowing the inclusion of descendants of *any* person who had been recorded as a Mountain, Forest, or Fishing "Lapp" in historical property, taxation and population registries. That means that a person could be considered to be a Sámi if they could prove they had an ancestor marked as a "Lapp" (Finnish *lappalainen*), perhaps some 150 years ago - but they no longer had to have the additional bond to Sámi culture by "feeling themselves to be a Sámi".

The Sámediggi demanded the new definition be removed and returned to the one based on language and ethnic origin through language. In this definition a Sámi is identified as "a person who feels oneself as a Sámi, provided that they or one parent or grandparent spoke Sámi as their mother tongue, or that one parent is listed in the voter registry of the Sámediggi."

The language criteria are important - not just for the sake of language - because through the language a person becomes connected to the Sámi cultural heritage. The language is one of the most important unifying elements of solidarity in a society.

The position taken by the Sámi is that, although defining a Sámi is difficult, it is not arbitrary. The purpose of the ethnic group must be addressed through the dynamic relationship among the people - not archival research.

Sámi identity is not a question only of language, only of livelihood, only of living in Sápmi, or only of a way of life. The question is about a much deeper cultural unity, of belonging to a particular heritage of kin, language, and a whole cultural complex extending throughout Sápmi and going back in time.

Following generally accepted definitions, conditions and prerequisites for ethnicity are a common origin and culture, interactions and identity as an ethnic group, and "distinctiveness" as a people. The latter means that "We" are different from "Them". Ethnic identity results when members of a certain group have an awareness of their common difference in relation to other groups. They experience the same shared culture and the same shared identity that is different from other peoples. The connection of members to one another is characterized by spiritual kinship: the spirit of unity and loyalty.

Knowledge of a common origin includes, in addition to ancestry, a knowledge of the history and

Goahti **and apartment block at a City Sámi event in Helsinki. Photo: Jorma Lehtola.**

traditions. They have a powerful emotional impact. As an example, ancestral background is the most important aspect for the awareness of spiritual kinship among Sámi living in cities. It is this particular element that distinguishes their ethnicity, giving them a feeling of belonging together on the basis of biology. To that is linked the knowledge of a common heritage and language, all of which strengthens the togetherness of "Our" community as "We" and distinguishes "Us" from "Them", the Others.

Language and ancestry are examples of *objective* definitions of Sámi identity. The standpoint of Sámi, as well as other aboriginal peoples is, however, that *subjective* definitions are more important in the final analysis. There are more

important sides to this. First, individual self-identification - identification with a group - is an essential condition of belonging to a people. Second, the community tends to evaluate, from its own standpoint, who belongs within its sphere.

The United Nations' Human Rights Commission and, in particular, the ILO Convention No. 169 on indigenous populations accept the principle that an aboriginal people admits its own members. Sámi themselves define and decide who is a Sámi. That has been the custom used throughout the ages; Sámi have always known what being Sámi is in relation to others. Today this is publicly acknowledged on a legal basis, as well.

A CULTURE LINKED WITH NATURE

The Sámi have always relied on nature. Nature has provided the sources for both their material and spiritual culture. This base sets Sámi culture apart from industrial or agricultural civilizations. The relationship with Nature is not one-sided. Throughout centuries of adapting to varying natural conditions the Sámi left their "cultural mark" on the physical environment.

The internal differentiations in Sámi culture have been influenced by the diverse natural conditions of northern Fennoscandia. Sápmi contains many different types of landscape. The wide northern coniferous zone extends from northern Sweden and Finland all the way to the Kola Peninsula. The northernmost part of Sápmi is defined by the shores of the Atlantic and Arctic Oceans. Between the coniferous zone and the coast lie highlands of gentle fells and the rugged Caledonian mountain ridge.

This diverse natural environment induced different sources of livelihood and formed physical boundaries between groups of Sámi. The distinctions that evolved are apparent today: distinct languages, recognizable cultural characteristics, manifestations and attributes, as well as types of livelihoods. A common thread for all Sámi groups is the adaptation of their way of life to the yearly cycle of nature and to the specific local natural environment.

Sápmi provides livelihood under natural environmental conditions that can support a limited population. Therefore, the numbers of Sámi have always remained reasonably low. Because their way of life is based on respect for Nature, Sámi have been very frugal in their use of natural resources. They seldom changed their environment radically, for example, as neighboring cultures have done through logging, mining or damming rivers.

However, as communities grew, over-exploitation sometimes occurred. That happened in the Middle Ages in connection with hunting wild reindeer and possibly earlier, in the Iron Age, with whale and seal hunting along the coast.

Sámi religious belief reflected this close link with nature. According to the traditional Sámi beliefs, the world was inhabited by spirits. Human beings could only successfully make their living by cooperating with the natural forces. It was essential not to damage nature, as that would interfere with the higher spirits. The religious practices were cyclical, respecting the pattern of seasonal migration and the cycle of nature.

A thorough knowledge of nature enables Sámi to keep up a livelihood based on seasonal migrations and a diversified economy. The migration patterns were purposefully planned and managed; Sámi society was very well organized by the *siida*, a community of family groups who share and govern a jointly owned territory.

The Sámi have gently used nature to serve their needs. As times changed they adopted new technology and new livelihoods such as herding reindeer, raising goats and sheep and generally engaging in small-scale hay-dairy farming. At times of crisis the society had to adapt and evolve. For example, lack of game or population growth in the area may have led to overhunting and exhausting the stock of wild reindeer. The rise of reindeer herding was a reaction to the lack of game.

Peasant societies moving into Sápmi attempted to control nature. This was in direct conflict with traditional Sámi world-views. The spread of a technical, industrial culture into Sápmi has created many problems. Forestry, hydro-electric power plants and reservoirs, mining, recreation and conservation all compete for the use of nature in the same place at the same time.

The needs of a small population are generally overlooked. This is why ownership of land and waters in the North is a crucial issue for the future of Sámi and Sápmi. Outsiders have assumed control over natural resources that Sámi have relied upon - it is very controversial whether there is a satisfactory legal base for these circumstances. Many Sámi believe that the balance between people and Nature can be restored only by respecting the knowledge gleaned by Sámi living close to nature through the ages.

Gárena Biera or Piera Tornensis, 80, from Giehtaruohtas in 1950s. Photo: Marja Vuorelainen. Lapin maakunta-
museo.

Legalized language

One of the main demands in the Altá Conflict, the recognition of the status of the Sámi language and its protection in Norway, was realized fairly well by means of a language law passed in 1990. It was the first Sámi language law anywhere. Through it six municipalities in northernmost Norway became officially bilingual: Unjárga, Deatnu, Kárášjohká, Porsáŋgu and Guovdageaidnu in Finnmark Province, and Gáivuotna in Troms Province.

The fact that the language law applies to only six municipalities is strongly criticized: the South Sámi language areas were not included. Nevertheless, the enactment of the law means that Sámi and Norwegian have equal status in connection with all services. The law has been best fulfilled in Guovdageaidnu and Kárášjohka.

Municipal officials are required to know the Sámi language. Schools and day cares have become bilingual. Nowadays Norwegians even want their children to attend Sámi language day cares and schools; parents clearly feel that learning Sámi is a benefit since it is an official language.

In Norway the language law is more radical than the one of 1992 in Finland, which only recommends that officials and teachers know a Sámi language. Anyone has the right to use Sámi with authorities, who nevertheless are not obligated to learn Sámi even in Sápmi, the Sámi Home Area. If an official cannot speak Sámi, interaction takes place through an interpreter. The Sámi Language Office of the Sámediggi provides interpretation and translation services.

The Sámi language law in Finland is thus not based on Sámi proficiency or bilingualism in an administrative area, as it is in Norway. Therefore it promotes neither the use of the spoken nor the written language. Neither does providing services in Sámi secure the language well enough. Nevertheless the law gives the Sámi language a better status than it had before - an official standing. As such it makes for a more favourable atmosphere and positive attitudes.

Although the law is closely based on principle, its existence has created belief in the future, especially among young people. The older population's undervaluing of its own language has decreased. That has already been seen in the desire of Sámi to learn their mother tongue and in the efforts of officials and other outsiders to acquire skills in the Sámi language.

An important step forward in the language policy came in 1997 with long-term language day cares. Their goal is to help Anár and Skolt Sámi children to learn their own mother tongue before they begin school. First designed for the Maori, the aboriginal people of New Zealand, the language day cares are a type of preschool where skilled members of the aboriginal people teach their language and culture to children under school age. Instruction is through play and song and other stimulating activities. The parents' role in daily use of the mother tongue is also stressed.

On the Norwegian side, a daring reform came in 1997 with the introduction of a Sámi curriculum followed by schools in the Sámi area. In addition to language, Sámi culture is part of the school program. The curriculum is a serious move toward discussion on how the schools can support the development of Sámi identity. The curriculum iń Norway also takes Sámi identity more into consideration than earlier.

In Sweden, a Sámi language law has not yet been achieved. Without that the Sámi language really does not have official status either in offices or in schools. Because of the lack of respect the formation of identity of non-reindeer herding Sámi, above all, becomes clouded. In Swedish Lapland they number around 15,000, and research showed that in 1975, 40 percent could not speak Sámi. The lack of a language law further worsens the situation.

Most Sámi are naturally bilingual. Nowadays bilingualism is considered a valuable asset and a skill which is more common in the world than unilingualism. Learning the mother tongue is nonetheless the key to acquiring a foreign language better. But a living bilingualism requires improving the position and status of the minority languages. The goal of Sámi language instruction is to make it possible for a child to grow up to become a versatile bilingual individual.

Communications media

Sámi communications media - newspapers and electronic messaging - have been important to the society in two ways. The main feature is that they have developed the Sámi language and given it prominence. A good example is the oldest newspaper in the Sámi language: *Nuorttanaste* (Eastern Star, established in 1898), a religious paper published in Unjárga and printed in Čáhcesuolu in Norway. It has been outstanding spiritually in addition to being good for the language. It gave Sámi experience reading their mother tongue. During the difficult times of the Norwegianization policy, it brought forth the Sámi language as a written language.

The history of the Sámi communications media describes how they created it as well as how it reflected on Sámi identity. It is impossible to measure the importance to the identity of the Sámi people of such newspapers as *Sagai Mui'talægje*, *Lapparnes Egen Tidning*, and *Waren Sardne* (see section on "Awakening of Sápmi").

In general, among aboriginal peoples, the communications media and its relation to identity is well known. When aboriginal peoples grew out of small societies using oral communication, wider communication channels became necessity. Keeping a group informed is not merely a matter of transferring information, but is about building a society as well. The media creates "a common presence" for the people who do not necessarily know each other, but who feel like they belong together.

Of the present Sámi language newspapers (or magazines) the oldest, besides *Nuorttanaste*, are the bilingual *Samefolket* (The Sámi People, est. 1918) appearing on the Swedish side, and *Sápmelaš* (The Sámi, est. 1934) on the Finnish side. Founder Torkel Tomasson's successors kept *Samefolket* alive despite constant economic difficulties. Although Gustav Park, one of the early editors, represented the clergy, the paper's editorial policy was especially well-rounded. It paid attention to the interests of Reindeer Sámi and Southern Sámi alike. It contained news items, critical views, and extensive articles on culture, Sámi politics and people in general.

A selection of Sámi newspapers.

In the beginning, *Sápmelaš* (as of 1993 *Odda Sápmelaš* [The New Sámi]) stressed short news items, educational articles, and was highly literary. Many poems and prose, which would otherwise have had difficulty finding a forum, appeared in its pages. The present day paper ranges from news to long scientific articles. It has called attention to the conservation of natural resources and to Sámi political reality. A supplement to the paper *Anaraš* (The Aanaar Sámi) appears three times a year in the Aanaar Sámi language.

On the Norwegian side, *Ságat* (The News) was established in 1956, and began as a monthly paper; later twice a month. In the 1970s the Norwegian Workers' Party "commandeered" the paper, fired the editor-in-chief Odd Mathis Hætta, who was thought to be too political in Sámi matters, and made the majority of its owners become Nor-

91

wegian. The paper's editorial policy began to stress a position opposed to the *Norgga Sámiid Riikkasearvi* (NSR) representing Sámi opinion.

Ságat opposed the idea of Sámi cultural self-government, and during the Altá Conflict it emphatically presented a conciliatory position toward the interests of the Norwegian State. Some of its backers are very active in the Samediggi, and for that reason the paper has lately emphasized the "Sámi Spirit" and has held opinions firmly in favour of Sámi organizations.

Reacting to *Ságat*'s change of policy - similarly the demise in 1978 of the Sámi political newspaper *Nordkalott* (North Calotte) - Sámi organizations began to plan new newspapers. In 1978 the first issue of *Sámi Áigi* (Sámi Times) appeared, a weekly tabloid. With financial support from the Sámi organizations, the paper had an excellent start coinciding with the Álltá Conflict, which it especially actively supported.

In 1993 *Sámi Áigi* went bankrupt. Several months later *Min Áigi* (Our Times) followed in its footsteps in the same vein, appearing twice a week. Six months later, in competition with the Kárášjohka based *Min Áigi*, *Aššu* (Embers) was established in Guovdageaidnu, which was secured by State financial aid just as was *Min Áigi*.

In the most recent decades, a surprising number of Sámi newspapers have appeared, but often they have been short-lived. There is a wide spectrum of writings: religious and cultural papers, publication of Sámi political activities and conservative publications, newspapers to suit the tastes of adults, children and teenagers, magazines and yearbooks. The first of these was *Goaikkanasat* (Drops, 1978), which soon changed to a magazine type journal.

Among the collection are cultural newspapers such as *Áiti* (Storehouse, 1979) which only published one issue. Newspapers changed their content and appearance. It is hard to say whether some appeared as one issue or several, for example, on the Norwegian side *Sápmi* and *Charta 79*, or on the Swedish side whether *Vuovjjuš* was a thematic review, a journal or a members' magazine. Their fates were similar, however. For example, the children's paper *Mánáid Bladdi* (The Children's Magazine) went bankrupt.

In the 1990s several lively special papers appeared - they also were "naturally" on the Norwegian side. The newspaper *Š* is a colourful publication that deals with the problems of youth as well as their dreams. It is published by Iput Press three times a year. Equally impressive is the women's paper *Gába* (Woman) established in 1996, which appears as a bilingual issue in Sámi and Norwegian. Among other things, it has published articles about blending the traditional with the life of today's Sámi women. Very early on, the Sámi press began using electronic communication in Sámi languages, and many have electronic versions on the worldwide web.

The growth of a Sámi feeling of community has been made possible through technological innovations, above all electronic media like radio. Radio overcomes distances and borders in a new way. Radio is irreplaceable for developing the language and creating new expressions. By activating Sámi mother tongue, radio protects it against the overwhelming force of the national languages.

The history of Sámi radio goes back more than 50 years. The Norwegian radio began regular broadcasts in the Sámi languages from Romsa (Tromsa) in 1946. Two years later a permanent programme secretary position was created, and the broadcasting location changed to Čáhcesuolu. In 1959 a new position was filled by Kathrin Johnsen, who was named "the Mother of Sámi radio", and she produced programmes for the next 30 years.

On the Finnish side, there may have been sporadic programmes as early as 1946, but regular broadcasting began the following year from Oulu. It consisted of news once a week and, very rarely, religious programmes. The *Samii Litto* organization had intentions to increase the programming, but the directors of the Finnish National Radio (*Yleisradio*) did not see the need until the end of the 1960s.

The Swedish radio Sámi programming was broadcast from Johkamohkki starting in 1953. Programmes mainly concerned reindeer herding and were in Swedish. The first Sámi language on Swedish national radio was located in Luleju in 1966 and four years later in Giron.

The concept of a common Sámi culture and a unified community was evident in Sámi radio productions. Development of cooperation across the national borders started in the 1960s. The most concrete result was the pan-Nordic news, which began broadcasting from Romsa (Tromsa) in 1964. Current programmes with a common interest to all the North Calotte countries was broadcast from Giron from 1973 to 1986, after which date the funds were redistributed.

Until 1965, the dream of a cooperative northern radio and television production centre was never achieved. Many committees had met to discuss the idea, which finally was given up in 1979. In 1986 the cooperative broadcasting also ceased. With the disused office in Giron and the shared funds that were to be divided, more jobs and more broadcast possibilities were created.

In 1970 there was a remarkable change in Sámi broadcasting. On the Finnish side, the head office was moved to Anár in Sápmi in 1973 and it was given a director and a Sámi speaking programming board. In 1977 their own studio and broadcasting facilities were built in Aanaar. The next year the Norwegian Sámi radio moved from Romsa (Tromsa) to Kárášjohka, also in the centre of Sápmi.

The Norwegian Sámi radio expanded greatly in the 1980s, because the State invested heavily in it to clear its tarnished reputation after the Álta Conflict. The Kárášjohka broadcasting centre grew quickly so that in 1992 there were 19 employees. The programming time rose to nearly 1800 hours yearly. The centre began regular television programming of current affairs and later children's programmes.

The Swedish headquarters did not fare so well. The producers did not demand nor receive enough independence. Sámi programmes were part of the programming for northern Sweden and were anywhere and anytime. In 1996 the Sámi in Sweden could hear programming in Sámi only 190 hours a year.

On the Finnish side, Sámi broadcasting increased in the 1970s to become a particularly strong influence in Sámi society. In addition to Northern Sámi, the radio produced programmes in Skolt Sámi and in Aanaar Sámi languages. In 1985 Sámi Radio became an independent regional radio with its own director under the management of the national radio. In the beginning of the 1990s Sámi Radio had 16 employees. The radio station has regional production in Gárasavvon and Ohcejohka.

Sámi programmes were produced for television especially in Sweden and Norway, beginning in the 1960s. Many special Sámi programmes were made, and in the 1990s Norwegian and Swedish television produced a decent regular series called *Arran* (The Campfire). Since 2000 Swedish, Norwegian and Finnish Television have collaborated to bring regular newscasts in Sámi.

In artistic handicraft old designs unite with new perceptions. *Solju*, a woman's brooch made by Petteri Laiti, silversmith from Aanaar. Photo: Petteri Laiti.

SÁMI ART - NEW AND OLD LIMITS

"Sámi artists differ from the artists of the majority populations in that they can not just sit in their studios producing works of art. They must participate in many activities. Sámi culture is at a stage where everyone needs to work to further Sámi politics, organizations, and culture. Artists also need to be engaged in order to develop and advance Sámi culture." So said Sámi artist and chair of the *Sámi Daiddačehpiid Searvi* (Association of Sámi Artists), poet Synnøve Persen, at the end of the 1980s.

Through their own activities, Sámi artists have had a great impact on cultural policies. They have participated in cultural community activities, established associations and worked in and through them, written polemic texts, voiced their opinions and organized demonstrations. With their own art they have strengthened and shaped a new Sámi identity, a self-image of Sámi people in the present transition.

An especially important turning point that was influenced by artists, and which influenced the artists in return, was the conflict over the damming of the Álta River. At this moment many of the most important and influential artists are former Álta activists: Rose-Marie Huuva, Synnøve Persen, Nils Utsi. Singer Marie Boine's eyes were opened to her own Sámi identity through Álta, though slightly later. *Beaivváš*, the Sámi theatre, produced their first musical on the theme of Álta.

Sámi artists have also broken through the borders of art forms carefully defined by western cultures. This is seen in Nils-Aslak Valkeapää's work. His multiple crossing of borders is based on the old world-view of a small people. Living on the borders of many cultures is reflected in their dynamic and flexible life concepts. Against this backdrop is the commitment of art to the normal necessities of life, as Valkeapää declared, "Sámi culture has never had art. It never had artists either. [...] Traditionally, to the Sámi everything was life; part of life is in nature, natural life."

The artists' diversity has also characterized their search for integration. In the 1970s and 1980s Sámi art tried to identify a feeling of Sámi self-awareness and personality in the transitional stage of the present times. How does one unite in spirit this culture that has been divided among different countries; how does one develop Sámi culture in the conditions of modern society; how does one treat the old Sámi cultural traditions and values using the language of the new world-view of young Sámi that they received in school? In clarifying one's own feelings, Sámi artists have often become the catalyst for the feelings of many of their compatriots.

The problems of Sámi born after the War are particularly painful because relating to their own culture is not at all self-evident. The background of many artists and writers is haunted by the conflict between their secure childhood environment and their school experiences. Common themes in literature are bitter images of boarding schools, many visual artists recognize that they are dealing with the trauma between childhood memories and modern times.

The turning point happened in the 1970s and 1980s. At that time, young Sámi, typically belonging to the first generation who attended schools and lived in boarding houses, began to rebel against assimilation and the vanishing of the old Sámi culture. Modern Sámi artists began to delve into their backrounds, expressing in their art the mental traumas and problems of self-image. Mari Boine has described this in the following words.

"When I began to make music I didn't think of myself as a 'musician' or an 'artist'. I just had the need to get out the painful things. My self-image was full of wounds and aches, and making songs was medicine for those. Only when people who heard the songs came and asked, 'how do you manage to tell so exactly about me and my feelings?' did I understand the songs were like medicine for others, too. The next step was that I wanted to make others understand us and our pain: those who had looked down on us and had diminished and wounded us. The third step was to notice how great were the riches and traditions contained in our culture. I wanted to bring out the way of thinking that we, and other aboriginal peoples, have. And I tried to say that this thought pattern has become important for the whole world which is poisoning and destroying the environment forever."

Artists have created their works in the cross currents of many kinds of influences. They have had to discover their relation to the age-old shamanistic traditions, often only seen and read in books, and to their predecessors in art at the beginning of the 20th century. Many visual artists are traditional artisans, masters adept at handicrafts passed down through tradition, and skilled yoikers; but perhaps even more have learned their art in modern schools. Writers have adopted in school the literary values of the majority population; leading visual artists have attended respectable art schools and art academies; musicians have absorbed influences from western pop music and world music.

In Synnøve Persen's opinion there is no reason to try to weed out the influences of western art because they are in any case at the base of every Sámi's education. Instead it would be important for Sámi studying in schools and other educational institutions to relate the majority population's art instruction to their own tradition and identity. The major problem for Sámi visual art, in Persen's opinion, is that in their own art language the bridge or jumping off point, by which to create varying models and above all to push against and to set excep-

tions, has been missing. In literature the problem is the same: how does one combine the ways of oral tradition into a form that will still interest today's reader.

Literature and modern times

Sámi traditions of word-smithing are strong. For instance, the shores of the Deatnu, from where the largest number of Sámi writers has come, are known in tales and memoirs as the "Homeland". The traditional myths and tales have been transmitted mainly in children's literature. Literature for adults features more stories about daily life, memoirs of great personalities and interesting events.

Biographical material is an essential part of Sámi literature; a documentary tone is characteristic in autobiographies as well as novels. A powerful genre, in addition to novels, is poetry. Its imagery returns in part to the yoik tradition. Yoiks with words were often also finely crystallized poems. The main features of the poetry are depictions of objects created through musical and verbal imagery.

Every young body of literature passes through a tendentious period in its development, in which it tries to strengthen its own identity against powerful forces of adversity. This is illustrated by the early works of Nils-Aslak Valkeapää and Kirsti Paltto, which were sharply worded polemics written in Finnish.

In the 1970s works of young Sámi writers were much published in newspapers and in anthologies. The most typical was Kirsti Paltto's poetry, in which all of the modern day problems brought into Lapland were rolled out before the reader: tourism, the vanishing Sámi culture, immigration, and unemployment. Paltto's style was straightforward, challenging, and at times ironic.

Paltto went on to become one of the most versatile Sámi writers. Since the beginning of the 1970s she has published children's books, poetry, short stories, novels, plays, radio plays, and treatises on Sámi culture. In her prose she covers a wide range of topics and times. In her large novels and short stories she has captured the old tradi-

Kerttu Vuolab

Ánde ja Risten Jagi fárus

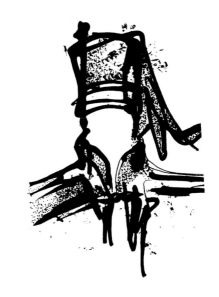

Sámi literature has been expanding over the last decades; here cover designs of works written by Kerttu
Vuolab and Rauni Magga Lukkari, Sámi women from
Finland. Drawing by Nils-Aslak Valkeapää, who also
designed the cover for Lukkari´s book.

tional tales of the earth spirits and *stállu*, the giant, as well as modern day topics, Sámi politics and the status of women.

Rauni Magga Lukkari's tone was softer from the very beginning. In her first collection of poetry she pictured, through the experience of youth in daily life, the Sámi's estrangement from and even relinquishing of their cultural identity. For Lukkari school signifies the separation from home and language and the transition to another world; coming from there to accept that the child come into conflict with the background, which reflects the whole culture. Lukkari describes, now delicately, now satirically, a young man giving up his Sámi identity and culture, seen from the viewpoint of the young Sámi woman who is in love with him.

Nils-Aslak Valkeapää's works from the 1970s crystallize many characteristic features of Sámi poetry of that decade. A central theme for Valkeapää was the conflict between the different mental worlds of a people close to nature and of western cultures. He stressed the language of Sámi experience in nature, and portrayed the difficulties of Sámi children in the strange environment of a Finnish school and their development of an understanding of the beauty of their own people's picture of life. But once again the language problem comes up: how can one accurately explain the Sámi way of thinking to someone who is seeing it on paper and through their own values? On a trip to visit North American Indians as a Sámi musician he found new hope when he realized that readers were to be found among the world's aboriginal peoples, whose problems were similar to the Sámi's.

Paulus Utsi, a Sámi from the Swedish side and most noted pioneer in the art of Sámi poetry, emphasized the meaning of language in expressing the affection for Sámi life. For him the language of a people close to nature forms a completeness with nature, and preserving the language is a fight for nature. Utsi's allegories are also connected directly to nature. He depicts the ancient Sámi culture in melancholic, gentle tones and words in which he stresses, above all, the meaning of work and creativity in every day tasks. The troubling sights of empty villages and "shoreless shores" appear as haunting nightmares in his poems.

As the self-esteem of Sámi culture clearly became invigorated during the 1980s, writers no longer needed to stress the problems of Sámi identity and being Sámi. The period of programmatic literature was coming to an end. Now Sámi identity started to mirror a deeper essence than merely defining it against the outside. Perhaps for that very reason the novel became the predominant form. In novels, writers tried to map the Sámi way of thinking and the conformity to law within the society. The literature of the 1990s particularly stressed the recent history of life in Sápmi since the war.

Hans-Aslak Guttorm's works were a link to the older Sámi literature. In 1941 he had published a small collection of short stories. Although he did not publish his other manuscripts, he influenced writers for half a century. When he retired from teaching in the beginning of the 1980s, he revised his old manuscripts into books. In his collections of short stories and short novels he depicts the daily life of people of the Deatnu at the beginning of the twentieth century. He writes humorous tales of bachelor Juoksa's foolish escapades in his surroundings and in the meeting of two cultures.

Whereas the old teacher Hans-Aslak described people of the Deatnu in his style of quiet empathy, his neighbour Eino Guttorm, a writer from the younger generation, painted a completely different picture of the people of Deatnu in the 1950s. Beginning with his first novel *Árbeeatnan luohti* (Song of the Inherited Land, 1981), he sharply pointed out the faults and shortcomings of his compatriots. He sees his own Sámi background as a bottled up community, in which people's relations to one another, even in Deatnu, are controlled by the general intolerance and double standards of Laestadianism.

In a series of novels, Kirsti Paltto set out to trace our own time still farther back into the 1930s. The two volumes that have been published so far, *Guhtoset dearvan min bohccot* (1987, Keep well, Our Reindeer) and *Guržo luottat* (1991, Tracks of Bad Spirits), are deeply descriptive of the mental turning points in Sámi culture: the impacts of the war and the evacuation. Paltto has chosen as the setting a small Sámi village whose members land in the sphere of influence of the strange national

Oahp'tii Hánsa, Hans-Aslak Guttorm, was a teacher at the Vuovdaguoihka school. During retirement he succeeded to continue his literary work that he began during his youth. Photo: Veli-Pekka Lehtola.

majority population and gradually come under their feet, too.

Events are described through the small boy Johanas, who grows up in a very different world than his parents. A certain fragmentation and "incompleteness" are distinctive traits of Sámi narration, as are the evocative characterizations of a large gallery of people. In the first volume of the series the contrasts between Sámi and Finns are expressed; in the second, Sámi relations to each other are portrayed. The works entertain through the aspects of their positive heroes, but people's jealousy, laziness and greed are also brought forth.

In Paltto's manner, Rauna Paadar-Leivo's novel *Goalsenjárga* (1994, Merganser Point) looks at the postwar period in Sápmi through the eyes of youth. It is concerned with young Biret-Anni's problems of self-esteem at the family level. The evacuation, her father's death and her mother's new boyfriend mean that the girl is constantly having to give up a previous way of life and readjust to new circumstances. Her relationship with her mother becomes a central theme of the book, while the character of the family's despised aunt serves as a contrast to Biret-Anni's feelings.

Jovnna Ánde Vest's debut work *Čáhcegáddái nohká boazobálggis* (1988, The Reindeer Path Ends at the Water's Edge) is set between the 1950s and 1970s. It is a biography of the author's father, a portrayal of the love-hate relationship between father and son; at the same time, it is a picture of the years of change within the whole culture. Vest's hold is now humorously tender and affectionate, now quite ironic and critical. The criticism extends to the general image of Sámi.

People living amid nature, especially in ethnographic portrayals, are usually seen as being steadfast, traditional, practical, and narrowminded; Vest's portrayal is completely different. His hero and anti-hero "Little Vest" is a Sámi from Deatnu, who, in the place of daily work, is fascinated by everything new and impractical just like a small child. The idealistic father's impractical yearnings compressed into hard reality create a pleasant, but true picture of the crisis in Deatnu in the 1950s.

Kerttu Vuolab's novel *Čeppari čáráhus* (1994) also describes the 1950s, the time of school and boarding house traumas, but it is not so strongly bound in time. Rather than a message of Sámi ideology, the spotlight is on the psychological growth and development of the main character. The novel tells of growth out of despair; of the loss of and search for security. Vuolab's portrayal of the main character is not one of a self assured, reliable hero figure whose role is to get Sámi to realize their national political position. She is by all means a hero, not by overturning the unavoidable realities of life, but rather by triumphing over her own confusion and insecurity. Curious episodes of dreams and fantasy give an otherwise realistic tale an unusual tone.

Besides treating the postwar years, Sámi prose has lately expanded into the turning points of more recent history. Going out into the world and relating to one's home region while living abroad has become a central theme. It is significant that in some of Vest's later novels there is no longer any mention of Sámi identity. They are novels of inner development set in unfamiliar environments, linked to Sámi culture only by the language. In their form they depict life's disintegration as in a broken mirror. In later novels, Vest has again moved back to Deatnu and recent history.

More concrete relations between his own and foreign cultures are brought forth in Olavi Paltto's short story collection *Juohkkásan várri* (Shared Hill, 1995). It portrays immigrants: Chileans, Savo people, blacks and Sámi come together and meet in the *Exilium* Restaurant. The work tells of rootlessness and breaking ties and also of finding them again. The title refers to the people being divided between two positions in life: the one of lost past habits and the other of new unattainable ones.

Narratives of life have remained an important part of Sámi literature. Good examples are Ilmari Mattus' *Eellimpäälgis* (Life's Path, 1996) and *Čovčjäävrist Kaamasan* (From Čovčjäävri to Kaamas, 1996) which describe an Aanaar Sámi youth's life after the war. Iisakki Paadar's collection of short stories *Issá muitala* (Issá Narrates, 1995) contains witty and charming memories of people and unbelievable events.

In the same way that novels sought new directions in the 1980s, so did Sámi poetry, reaching deeply into the world of Sámi feelings and life. The wave of Sámi ideological struggling was past and,

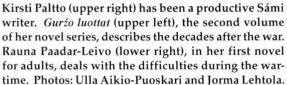

Kirsti Paltto (upper right) has been a productive Sámi writer. *Guržo luottat* (upper left), the second volume of her novel series, describes the decades after the war. Rauna Paadar-Leivo (lower right), in her first novel for adults, deals with the difficulties during the wartime. Photos: Ulla Aikio-Puoskari and Jorma Lehtola.

apparently consciously, the change was to short, meditative poems bringing out the psychological, sensitive inner feelings of the common person.

The most important lyricist has been Rauni Magga Lukkari, in whose new works the analysis of women's feelings has replaced more general Sámi themes. With cheerful irony she has portrayed the contrasts and love-hate relationships between women and men and between generations. Life's cycle is portrayed from two viewpoints, the child's and the mother's.

The second notable Sámi woman lyricist at this moment, Inger-Mari Aikio, has also drawn away from depicting opinionated or traditional views of Sámi cultural identity. She writes poems in which the inner feelings of young women are clothed in the sensitive tone of a spirited Sámi language. The countryside and life in Sápmi blend with impressions of modern times. As a counter weight to the traditional way of thinking centred around kin and family, Aikio's poems often map a person's inner self. They portray strong emotions: jealousy, love, the emptiness of separation and solitude.

Resembling Aikio, Synnøve Persen, in three collections of poetry, has depicted people's inner feelings crystallized through images of nature. Stina Inga, a young Sámi from the Swedish side, uses sparkling colours of life: "the lustre of blue light and white snow tinged with disappointed love". Artist Inghild Tapio's didactic narrative poetry covers aphoristic views of life in general, nature and the mysterious side of people.

In contrast to the short forms these women poets used, Nils-Aslak Valkeapää, in his epic poem, ambitiously tried to create a complete picture of the entire Sámi people's world of thought and traditions. A more psychological balancing of accounts is found in his earlier works, collected in the trilogy *Ruoktu váimmus* (Home in the Heart, 1985). The trilogy is the story of one person, of the whole Sámi people, and of an entire way of life. The image of a Sámi child growing up is shaped into a poetic view of the clash between the two cultures and two ways of thinking.

Whereas the poetry of *Ruoktu váimmus* resembles lyrical yoiks, *Beaivi, Áhčážan* (The Sun, My Father, 1988) reveals the structure of an epic yoik. It has symphonic proportions combining mythi-

cal, historical and personal themes into an artistic whole: the work operates on the levels of language, history and mythology.

Because it is a work of poetry, the mythical and stylistic elements are essential, but the historical setting is also a distinguishing feature of the work. On the level of the individual, it is the story of one Sámi's life after the war; on the historical level it is a depiction of the whole past of the Sámi people; on the mythological level it tells of an artist noaidi, his dreams and the realities inherent in them. Valkeapää received the Nordic Literature Prize for his works in 1991.

The voice of the minority was heard more clearly in the 1980s. Stig Gaelok Urheim, a Luleju Sámi, in his collections *O, Oarjjevuodna* (Oh, Southern Fjord, 1983; the North Sámi word meaning "western" is "southern" in Urheim's dialect), *Vuonak = fra fjordene* (Fjords, 1986) and *Amuk ... den fremmende* (Amuk - The Stranger, 1988) highlighted the viewpoint of his home region Divttasvuotna, and criticized the dominance of North Sámi over other Sámi. A personal tragedy, his brother's suicide, led to another book *Ale desti! - ikke mer!* (No More!, 1992).

In another part of Sápmi, on the Kola Peninsula, poetry was also being created. Oktjabrina Voronova is considered the first Kola Sámi poet. She wrote poems in Ter Sámi and published them in local newspapers until her collection *Jella* (Life) appeared in 1989. She has published other collections in Russian. In her poetry, Voronova uses inspiration from nature and living with nature, often elevating these ideas into a philosophy of life: "We have power / because we eat a lot. Why then do we never fly?" Two books by Askold Bazanovin, written in Russian, have been translated into North Sámi.

Until the end of the 1980s, many authors writing in Sámi came from the Finnish side. Sámi authors on the Norwegian and Swedish sides were producing works, but often wrote in those national languages. In Norwegian literature, Ailo Gaup and Aagot Vinterbo-Hohr are very well-known; Vinterbo-Hohr received the coveted *Tarjei Vesaas* award for her *Palimpsest* (Palimpsest, 1987).

The biggest issue for Sámi literature is the limited readership leading to publication problems

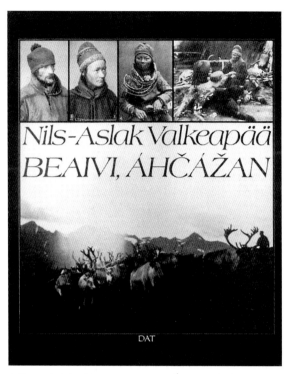

Nils-Aslak Valkeapää's *Beaivi, Áhčážan* (The Sun, My Father) is a multi-level representation of Sámi history and mental landscape. The Sámi language version is enriched by a large collection of pictures.

The Russian language collection of poems by Oktjabrina Voroneva was published after her death.

that have caused many Sámi publishing houses to go bankrupt. The strongest and most successful and experienced publisher is *Davvi Girji o.s.* (The Northern Book) in Kárášjohka, which is a limited company funded by the municipality of Kárášjohka and the Sámediggi. It publishes general literature as well as textbooks. Other active publishers on the Norwegian side are *Iđut* (Swells) in Porsáŋgu and *DAT* in Guovdageaidnu. The publisher on the Swedish side is *Sámi Girjjit* (Sámi Books) in Johkamohkki. On the Finnish side, until the 1990s, *Girjegiisá* (Book Box) was the main publishing house for literature, and *Gielas* (The Keel) also issued some books. Since the beginning of 2000, there have been no permanent Sámi publishers on the Finnish side, and Lapin sivistysseura, which was responsible for seeing that literature in Sámi was published in Finland, no longer publishes.

THE NEW VOGUE IN HISTORICAL WRITING

In the summer of 1995 there was a special ceremony at the cemetery on Lake Aanaar's (Anár) sacred island. Ten human skulls were blessed and consecrated to their final resting place. These skulls were the remains of Sámi forefathers which had been collected in Sápmi in dubious circumstances in the early 1900s. In the 1930s a group of Finnish anthropologists dug up 77 Sámi skeletons from the cemetery. In 1998 in Bossegohppi, Norway, a similar ceremony was held when the skulls of the two people condemned to death for their part in the Guovdageaidnu Uprising were finally consecrated (see earlier section).

Sámi museums such as Ajtte in Johkamohkki and Siida in Aanaar (Anár) exhibited old Sámi items that had been in European museums. Among the items displayed were old noaidi (shaman) drums and silver jewellery that the renowned archaeologist Arthur Evans had excavated from the sacred cemetery island of Lake Anár (Aanaarjávri) in the 1800s.

The awakening of Sámi historical consciousness was kindled by the discussion that arose at the end of the 1980s about returning "stolen" artifacts. Besides bones and skulls, huge numbers of other items had been taken to the South from the Sámi homeland: noaidi drums, sieidi (shrine), jewellery and items of everyday art. Even Sámi intellect had been used as a source of raw data: their knowledge had been archived in collections that researchers used to build their own careers.

The general trend was that Sámi possessions that had been taken in the name of archaeological or ethnographic research were not returned to the Sámi. When Sámi artist Nils-Aslak Valkeapää was searching for pictures of Sámi for his epic *Beaivi, Áhčážan* (1988, The Sun, My Father; Trekways of the Wind, 1994) he found hundreds and thousands, as far away as Paris - most were unknown to the Sámi. In his work Valkeapää returned the pictures as a kind of family album.

There is a personal challenge, especially for writers of Sámi history. They must also endeavour to "return" the archives of the Sámi's own background so that Sámi can understand them from their own vantage point.

The right to one's own history

It has only been in recent decades that the Sámi's own perspective in historical research has come strongly to the fore. The reality of present Sámi politics provided the stimulus; the Sámi Instituhtta (Nordic Sámi Institute) began an extensive legal history project in the 1970s. Its aim was to establish a picture of Sámi rights to land and water in their own area, based on historical and scientific methods. The most notable achievement of that project was Kaisa Korpijaakko's doctoral thesis completed in 1989, in which she clearly shows that Sámi land ownership practices in the 1600s were comparable to the property laws of the Scandinavian countries. Indeed, other historical studies by Sámi have been carried out in connection with the active Sámi political and cultural movements.

During the controversy over protection of the Álta River, at the turn of the 1980s, Sámi themselves began scientific searches for relevant fixed points in their own history: the Strömstad Border Treaty of 1751 guaranteed special rights for Sámi; this treaty drew the border in northern Scandinavia between Norway and Sweden, thus dividing the Sámi territories; the treaty, which the Sámi refer to as the Sámi Magna Charta assured their rights to continue their nomadic cycles across the border. The only rebellion in Sámi history was the Guovdageaidnu Uprising of 1852, which was upheld by some people as a symbol during the Álta Conflict. Sámi began using the name Sápmi for their homeland when the Sámi settlement area began to disintegrate because of being split among four countries. An historical step in Sámi political history was the Sámi Conferences, composed of Sámi from all four countries. These are just a few of the historical events illuminated from the Sámi viewpoint by these researches.

Typical of Sámi historical research conducted by Sámi is that it struggles to establish general overviews and outlines, like Samuli Aikio's *Olbmot ovdal min* (1992, The People Before Us). Sámi researchers also stress micro-history and the significance of kinship. They describe important periods of transition like the change in land ownership rights, the relationship between the old Sámi religion and Christianity, trade relationships, the changes brought about by World War II and the ensuing evacuation, and the language crisis faced by Sámi due to increased assimilation into the national majorities or State societies.

Activism and adaptable Sápmi

The trend of Sámi being directed to their own history was stimulated in part by discussions in recent decades among the world's aboriginal peoples. In this setting questions have been raised, such as "the right to one's own history". The premise is that the ideology of development of the majority populations has influenced the whole picture of aboriginal peoples and their past.

Historians in the Nordic countries have begun to recognize openly that interpretations may differ greatly even when they are based on the very same sources from the same archives. There is, at the same time, an awareness that these different interpretations are the basis for researchers and schools to make decisions about which historical events are important. Ideas receive wide support from those groups in society to whose aims they best correspond.

The basis of the traditional picture of Sámi history is the research of "lappologists" who worked from the turn of the 20th century until the 1950s. Its basis was the mentality and attitudes of the recent colonists: the idea of improving agricultural society. According to this mind-set, natural peoples had remained behind in their cultural development. The primitive traits of Sámi culture were emphasized and Sámi passivity, as well. They were sacrificed to the more aggressive ways.

Certain basic concepts circulated from one study to the next and became myths. A good example of historical writing founded on myths is precisely that idea that Sámi had no concept of land ownership. Korpijaakko explains in her exceptional research into the beginnings of this idea that none of the scientific literature was based on sources - let alone the actual practices. The idea just somehow

The first general treatment of the own past as a people written by a Sámi was Samuli Aikio's *Olbmot ovdal min* (**The People Before Us, 1992**). It draws a picture of the Sámi as active and powerful individuals and as a group in the past, who knowingly cared about their society's balance and development in relation with neighbouring cultures. **Photo: Kalle Kuittinen.**

became widespread and thereby became "the truth", and no one ever thought to scrutinize or verify this "truth" in their research.

When historical events are examined from the Sámi's own vantage point, the Sámi become the centre of the events and at once the picture of a passive and sacrificing existence changes. Historical research by Sámi reveals that Sámi are characteristically an active, functional group with a clear knowledge of their possibilities to have an impact on their own situation, even within the Nordic system. Therefore "Sámi political activism" has become a central theme for research.

The Sámi's own opinion emphasizes a strategy that is different from the majority population's. Rather than being war-like, seeking political power and controlling nature, the Sámi way of acting has been marked by traditions of peaceful trade, living in contact with many cultures and an extraordinary ability to adapt and to absorb new influences and pressures without losing their "Sámi self".

Music between tradition and the stage

Yoik, hymn, melody, rock, country, jazz, orchestra, symphony, ethnomusic ... In the past few decades Sámi music has gone through the whole spectrum of western musical forms from one end to the other. This experimentation created an explicitly Sámi music thanks to Sámi language, Sámi themes and the yoik tradition.

The development of Sámi music in the 1970s and 1980s followed the same course of development as other areas of Sámi art. Its central aspect was also a problem: the conflict between new influences and the old tradition. How could one combine the yoik tradition with new musical forms? The 1960s had created a "boarding house generation" of Sámi, who had spent the greater part of their youth, usually from the age of seven, in the boarding house environment hundreds of kilometres from home.

The youth were used to listening to the radio and to western music, its melodies and instruments. The yoik no longer was enough for them. Many thought it monotonous and old-fashioned compared to western music ideals. Nevertheless, the yoik has been a powerful inspiration for many musicians; the yoik tradition runs in the veins of musical Sámi. Heikki Laitinen, music researcher, has shown that it has been preserved in Sámi music surprisingly strongly up to the present day. The mutual influence of these two musical forces, western and yoik, gave Sámi music in the 1970s and 1980s its own distinctive mark.

The yoik represents the clearest of all the age-old Sámi cultural traditions. Yoik music is said to be "the world's most aboriginal song form", something of the most ancient cultural layers of humankind or, at least of northern peoples. The object of a yoik may be nature, animals, often a person; it paints a picture using words, melody, rhythm, expressions and gestures of its performances. The characterization is often suggestive, condensing the object to some essential feature; the text is complemented by alliterative repetition, using small, but meaningful words. Yoik is said to remove distance: the friend who is gone is brought back through a yoik. In the comprehensive and personal nature of its feelings the yoik brings people together, creating solidarity. And that is precisely one reason for its preservation.

The yoik has always been one of the cornerstones of Sámi identity, a strong expression of Sámi distinctness. Yoik has been an aspect of "our people", "our" point of view. It is no wonder that, in its attempt to break down the Sámi belief system and world-view, the church attacked yoiking. As well as forbidding spiritual yoiking, it also forbade normal, secular yoiks merely because of their distinctiveness.

Yoik retained a rebellious spirit, however. It was based on a quality of double-meaning, a certain ironic ambiguity - a code. Sámi researcher Harald Gaski points out that the epic yoiks of the 1800s contained clear political standpoints, but under the surface. For example, the yoik "The Thief and the Noaidi" works on two levels so that the Sámi community understood its content differently than outsiders like ministers and researchers.

On religious grounds, yoik has been disapproved even among Sámi up to the present day. To the Laestadian movement yoiking was a sin. It is said that the devil fallen from heaven yoiked. The Laestadian background of many of today's musicians has meant that they did not learn the yoik tradition naturally while they were growing up.

In the postwar years the yoik tradition was completely lost in some places, like the Anár region. However, even there it became a central symbol of the "Sámi renaissance". It may be said that Nils-Aslak Valkeapää's public performances, which began in 1966, raised yoik to a new flourishing and to a new identity as a symbol. Because of the possibilities given in its secret codes and concealed meanings, it is well suited as a weapon. Valkeapää brought together yoikers and organized large concerts, strengthening the status of yoiks. Sámi radio played yoik music liberally in its programmes.

The good yoikers have kept their position as artists ensuring the continuity of the tradition. Since the 1970s yoik recordings have continually appeared. Ingor-Ántte Áilu Gaup (Little Áilu), Inga Juuso, Piera Balto and Johan Anders Baer are some who have brought their skills in yoiking to compete with melodic instruments. Not to forget the

Many traditional yoik artists like Inga Juuso are from the area of the Reindeer Sámi in Norway. Photo: Jorma Lehtola.

The common cultural event of aboriginal peoples, *Davvi Šuvvá* (The North Sings) was organized the second time in 1993. Photo: Jorma Lehtola.

rarity of the 1980s, *Sámiid Eatnan* (Sámi Land), a yoik performed by Mattis Haetta in the Eurovision song contest. His entry is on the recording *Máze* (1982).

Individual yoikers, besides the Western Sámi, are found from Deatnu to Várjavuotna; Johan Andersen, from Várjavuotna, has delighted listeners with his imitations of animals and other sounds of nature in his performances. A more traditional album is Anne Marie Rasmussen's *Borjjastettiin ábi alde* (Sailing Across the Swamps, 1980), which contains spiritual music.

The minorities within the Sámi minority have had less representation, but also have gone in many directions. The singing traditions of Anár Sámi are presented by Aune Kuuva, Ilmari Mattus, Anja West and Petri Rautio. From among the Kola Sámi the song and dance group *Oijar* represented Soviet style folk art and, while not all of their members were Sámi, they made Kola Sámi known at international music festivals. Among their members were been excellent *leu'dd* singers, beginning with Maria Zakarova. Leu'dd, the special song form traditional to Skolt Sámi, resembles a ballad in that it tells a story, and can go on for hours when sung by the masters of the form, usually women.

Skolt Sámi leu'dd singers on the Finnish side have also been in demand: Tyyne Fofonoff, Vassi Semenoja and Helena Semenoff, who recorded *Sue'nn'jel lee'ud* (Memories of Sue'nn'jel, 1979). The most well-known Skolt Sámi musician is Jaakko Gauriloff, born in Nellim (Njellim, Njeä'llem), who developed music in the Skolt Sámi language in the "disco" style while he was a long time solo singer with a dance orchestra. One of his best known pieces is *Tanja* (1982).

Although yoik has preserved its age-old aspect and its personal nature in a remarkably large measure, it has also changed. Modern yoik is slightly more melodic, the use of the voice has become a bit more conventional, the words are fewer, especially in Western Sápmi. But it also has more infectious melodies and more lively rhythms. "Big Áilu's", Nils-Aslak Valkeapää's, way of developing yoik in the direction of today's western and world music has fascinated and appealed to many colleagues.

From yoik to ethnomusic

The expression of the new situation of music and its new influences in the 1970s was that music changed from participatory forms to a stage art. The yoik had been everyone's form; some of the better yoikers, of course, stood apart. In the 1970s, with active Sámi politics, music became part of official cultural programmes, expressly as concerts. Making recordings was also new; the first record made by a Sámi was Valkeapää's *Joikuja* (Yoiks, 1968); it still carried a Finnish title and was released by Otava, a Finnish publisher, as a literary recording.

The effect of stage art and recordings was that performances of yoik had to add rhythm and colour by using instruments. The first instrument to be adopted was naturally from the boarding schools: the guitar. *Dædnugátte nuorat* (Youth from the Shores of Deatnu), one of the most brilliant groups, brought drums and flutes as well as guitars onto the stage. They performed traditional yoiks in their concerts - some of the members of the group were masters of yoik - but also included European style tunes. The lyrics written by *Dædnugátte nuorat* were the elements that dominated Sámi music from then on: love of home, criticism of exploitation of nature and ballad-like songs of feelings. Two of the group's members, Irene Pettersen and Tore S. Aslaksen, started recording again in the 1990s.

Mainly inspired by *Dædnugátte nuorat* and Nils-Aslak Valkeapää, Sámi music entered a period of enthusiastic experimentation. *Máze nieiddat* (The Girls from Máze) put traditional yoik and new tunes together with tangos, polkas and the "Máze waltz". Ammun Johanskareng and Halvdan Nedrejord together developed pop and rock yoik. Country music began at one point to be the most Sámi of all Sámi music. Áilu Gaup's group *Ivnniiguin* played hard rock. Electric guitars entered the picture and synthesizers created the "Sámi sound" in the early 1980s.

Ammun Johnskareng, from Kárášjohka, was one of the most important musicians going into the 1980s, but his solo recording was not released until 1987. He had been a prominent performer of many genres at Sámi festivals and conferences.

Most popular were his mocking songs about Sámi politicians who tried to show they were Norwegians.

Johnskareng was a powerful man behind the scenes in the production of Sámi records. His debut record was made with *Hilda & Viddas Sønner* group in 1977. Another important group recording was *Guovssahaš*, which he established with Anne Jorid Henriksen, another prominent recording artist in the early 1980s. Henriksen's voice and performances held great expectations. However, she later turned more to the stage with *Beaivváš* theatre. Her place as a solo singer was filled by Mari Boine (formerly Persen).

Toward the end of the 1980s the duo *Sáve*, Ellen Vuolab and Magnus Vuolab, began to make Sámi disco music. Rock music has remained one of the main elements of Sámi youth culture; it was represented by such bands as *Intrigue* in Kárášjohka and *Orbina* and *Sánčuari* in Guovdageaidnu. Some theatre productions like *Beaivváš* theatre's rock musical *Earalagan* (Different, 1992) used influences of rock music.

Among many experimenters, Nils-Aslak Valkeapää (Áilu) generated a second peak for Sámi music after *Dædnugátte nuorat*. He produced records with other yoikers, optimistically reflecting a new spirit of the time. In his own works Valkeapää moved successfully among many musical forms: yoik, country, melodic, jazz, and others.

He experimented with song particularly in his record *Vuoi, Biret-Máret, Vuoi!* (1974), in which various western influences blended naturally to become part of the Sámi world of words and sound. In his concerts Áilu drew even closer to jazz's type of improvisational imagery and, above all, his collaboration with Seppo "Paroni" Paakkunainen brought extraordinary results. They produced long playing records *Sámi eadnan duoddariid* (1978), *Davás ja geassai* (1982), and *Sápmi, vuoi Sápmi!* (1982), in which guitarist Leo Gauriloff was an important artist.

His next recording *Sápmi lottážan 1-2* (Sápmi, My Dear Bird, 1992) went in a new direction, taking on new dimensions. Valkeapää clearly wrote it as a Sámi symphony. Musically and using special effects he was trying to present a complete picture of the Sámi world. Valkeapää combined many-voiced yoiks with sounds from nature and sounds that have a special meaning to the Sámi people, like police helicopters that are a reminder of the events at Álta. The CD images range from the barricades at Álta to New York. Also based on his book *Beaivi, Áhčážan* Valkeapää created three recordings with Esa Kotilainen. The last of these is a four CD set.

From the beginning, Valkeapää cast a musical background that is considered to have been a new phase in the ethnomusical sound of the 1980s. Besides yoiking with Áilu Gaup, Valkeapää often yoiked with Juhan Ánde Baer, for instance on *Dálveleaikkat* (Winter Games, 1992), the commemorative record for the Lillehammar Olympic Winter Games in 1994, and *Sámi Luondo, gollerisku* (Sámi Nature, Golden Ornament, 1992). He expanded his expression by using all the instruments of a symphony orchestra and finally sounds of nature. One of his most extraordinary musical achievements was *Goase dušše* (The Bird Symphony, 1993). For that work he was presented with the *Prix Italia* for the category of radio music in 1993.

Many Sámi musicians have come to yoik and other traditional music via western and ethnic music. Young musicians seldom have a completely natural relation to the yoik tradition. In addition to the school environment the main reason for that is their religious background in which yoiking was a sin. The best example is Mari Boine who grew up in Kárášjohka in the heartland of the Laestadian movement's influence, and who, in the 1990s, became the best known Sámi musician in the world.

Mari Boine grew up in a Laestadian family who disapproved of both yoiking and listening to radio. Her first musical experiences were singing hymns with the congregation. This influence can clearly be heard in her music and, above all, in the way she uses her voice. Her musical awakening came through listening secretly to pop and rock music on a neighbour's radio; these were the genres she aimed for as a young music maker.

The Álta Conflict also stirred Mari Boine, who was studying at the Álta teachers college at the turn of the 1980s. Through song, she began to examine the poor self-esteem of her own background, becoming an interpreter for many companions in misery. Her breakthrough came with her distinctive recording *Jaskatvuođa mannjá* (After the Silence, 1985). Its melodies and lyrics were typical of the young Sámi music of the 1980s: cloaked in rock, challenging, and even aggressively critical of society. The pieces placed blame with the "masters" for not listening and not understanding Sámi affairs; they prompted people to take a look at themselves as Sámi.

Shortly after the release of this first recording, her new singing style would be heard in concerts and "Sámi festivals". She felt herself walking on old noaidi paths. Her concerts captivated like shamanic meetings. Her song lyrics were like spells; problems were recognized, images were made of them and they were sung away. Her next recording *Gula gula* (Listen, Listen, 1989) was a breakthrough to international recognition; according to some critics, it was "unquestionably one of the best ethnomusic recordings ever produced in the Nordic countries".

Through world music Mari Boine came to her own style; her music integrates North and South American Indian music, rhythm, rock and roll, blues and jazz with Sámi music traditions. She criticizes "the White thieves'" contemptuous way of robbing everything exotic for themselves for colour, criticizes the rulers' way of stealing land by drawing borders on maps and appointing themselves as kings. On the other hand the lyrics show hope, "The boarding houses are crumbling / now we begin to find our way back / the law books are torn up / now we begin to find our way back."

Gula gula's softer, deeper tone came out clearly in Boine's later works. Now the main themes are the ancestors' mental world and heritage as a model for life, and a deep joy of life; these were expressed in the song "Here I am, blessed as a person". Mari Boine's musical hallmark is still the creation of a captivating magic through simple melodies and monotonal repetition.

As an unprejudiced musical exponent, Mari Boine resembles Valkeapää, who was her most important role-model. Boine's development went from rock to modern Sámi music to world music, then returned to her Sámi roots. In recent years she has taken up traditional yoiking. Although Boine took her main inspiration from the music of aboriginal peoples around the world, both Sámi and outsiders, she is considered a Sámi singer.

On the Finnish side, the best-known developers of Sámi music were Wimme Saari from Eanodat and the *Ánnel nieiddat* (The Girls from Ánnel) from Anárjohka. They represent the younger generation of yoikers who grew up in the new atmosphere proudly drawing from its Sámi heritage. Their performances reflect clearly their musical foundation in rock. "Through them yoik has broken down many barriers, filled rock and jazz clubs, been heard on radio and television and has visited schools," says a critic.

Wimme's background is to a certain extent the wrong way around. Growing up in a Laestadian family with ten children, Wimme learned early that whistling - to say nothing of yoiking - was a sin; it invited the devil. Working for the national radio (*Yleisradio*, Finland) as a sound control technician he was going through the collection of historical tapes and found recordings of yoik by his own relatives. They opened a new world to Wimme.

Wimme took traditional yoik into surprising directions: jazz improvisation and archaic yoiking. Just as he yoiked a wolf, a bear, or a person, he also yoiked an airplane engine, a snoring person's dreams or a short movie!

Especially fruitful was his work with the group *RinneRadio* led by Tapani Rinne. In their jazz compositions Wimme's yoiks were coloured with the voices of saxophone or computer music. For his solo recording the artist added special colour to his presentations with interesting backdrops of electronic effects: sound worlds which often had a humorous relation to the simplicity of yoik melodies.

The background of the *Ánnel nieiddat* is similar to Mari Boine's, with whom they studied at one time. In Ánnel, in the sphere of Laestadian awakening, the yoik tradition had partly vanished and the girls grew up more under the influence of western music. Their debut recording *Dolla* (Fire) in 1992 contains old, traditional yoiks and their own yoik compositions. The powerful use of drums and guitar made the group's performance so rhythmic and captivating that they became the leading name

Ulla Pirttijärvi, who earlier belonged to the Aŋŋel nieiddat, is making music on her own now. Photo: Jorma Lehtola.

in all Finland for ethnomusic and youth music. Ulla Pirttijärvi, a former member of the group, who later embarked on a solo career, is at this moment a leading Sámi musician. Her concerts also combine traditional yoiks and her own yoiks, which touch on very current themes, such as the plans for a mine in Áŋŋel. She also composed and wrote the lyrics to *Hoŋkoŋ Dohkká* (Hongkong Doll, 1996), a children's yoik collection that was released on CD and as a music book.

Alongside Mari Boine, among Sámi on the Norwegian side, the *Transjoik* (formerly the *Frode Fjellheim Jazz Yoik Ensemble*) has risen to international acclaim. Led by South Sámi Frode Fjellheim the group has arranged age-old yoiks from his ancestors in modern musical language.

Fjellheim, like Wimme, found the yoiks hidden away in archives. With recordings such as *Saajveh Dannhtsoeh* (Saiva's Dance, 1994) the group members used their backgrounds to take the yoiks into the direction of improvisation and jazz, achieving through tempo and voices a state of hypnotic trance.

111

Above: *Vilddas* - a group of young artists combining Sámi music and international influences.

Left: *Áŋŋel Nieidat* (Daughters of Áŋŋel) Ursula, on the back, and Tuuni Länsman. Photos: Jorma Lehtola.

Left: Since 1990 Wimme, projecting himself as a free artist, has created his own sound world in which humour is not lacking. His single *Texas*, when issued in 1996, rose to third place on the American ethnomusic chart, higher than the Macarena dance. Photo: Jaakko Heikkilä.

Below: Mari Boine is a well known Sámi musician. Her music echoes Sámi yoik tradition, Laestadian psalm chanting and world music. Photo: Jorma Lehtola.

113

DUODJI – HANDICRAFT

Handicrafts in Sámi culture have been shaped by the mobile lifestyle of seasonal rhythm and frugal use of nature, just as have other traditions. The hallmarks of the material culture are simplicity, frugality and practicality.

Sámi handicrafter Petteri Laiti points out that in traditional handicrafts aesthetics served use. A beautiful knife handle made of reideer antler would withstand use and wear. Curly birch, birch bark, or leather acted as shock absorbers between the antler pieces and eliminated the antler's tendency to slip from the hilt. When the maker adds abundant engravings they become elegant ornaments as well. The equally decorative sheath protects the blade so well that it could never harm the wearer. It was often made of bone because a leather sheath could be cut through when wrestling with a reindeer in the corral. The shape of a bone sheath is beautiful, but useful; it curves smoothly backward and has no notches that could catch on things. A hole directed toward the point of the blade, or many decorative holes, guides moisture away from the blade to keep it from rusting.

Craftspeople usually adapt themself to the materials rather than forcing the materials into a particular design or purpose. For example, a burl, which is used to make a *guksi* (drinking cup) or other vessel, must be hollowed out following its growth pattern and grain. The handle is made from the wooden stem clinging to the burl. Antler mountings or inlays are used as reinforcements and are also suitable for decorative engravings.

The combination of usefulness and beauty is pleasing to the eye. Ornamentation making bone and wood items appear valuable is known from as far back as the Stone Age. Ornamentation is an expression of the maker's own individuality and aesthetic ideas, which are forgotten with the passing of time. Sámi handicrafts are known for the beauty of their design, making them very desirable to outsiders.

In 1982 Sámi handicrafts acquired a trademark, *Sámi Duodji*, that identifies the work as genuine Sámi handicraft. Genuine handwork is made from traditional materials and uses traditional designs. It must be hand made, as the name implies. Though some machines may be used, for instance, in bone and wood work, the hand made nature of the work must be maintained.

Tradition in materials

Of the materials used in the most traditional, age-old Sámi handicrafts, the most important is wood: birch, pine and spruce. The bark of spruce, birch, alder and willow is used for colouring and the roots for making braided vessels. The next most important raw materials are from reindeer: hides, leather, antler and bone. During thousands of years Sámi learned to use nearly all parts of the wild reindeer and later reindeer from their herds. They used them sparingly for food and objects of use.

Some materials that were adopted at a later time in history and through trade with outsiders are also considered traditional, such as woollen broadcloth, silk, silver and tin. On the cutting edge of European cultural trends, especially in the period from 1300 to 1600, Sámi handicrafts took on many innovations, that later became hallmarks of Sámi culture.

The increased influence from the shores of the Arctic Ocean and Central Europe is seen above all in the use of silver. Possessions made of fur, fish and reindeer changed at the coast to silver spoons, dress ornaments and beakers. They were all purchased items made by silversmiths in cities. Silver was especially sought after for decorating belts and brooches, and for drinking vessels, necklaces and rings as well. From the start silver was linked to social status. It was also believed to have magic power.

At the end of the Middle Ages textiles came into use, mainly wool. They were obtained from neighbouring peoples. Most striking influences on the colourful Sámi garments came from the dress styles of Central Europe's upper classes. Wealthy Sámi may have traded for this clothing at the coast. Later when the dress had gone out of use in Central Europe, it spread and became the Sámi style of dress.

The origin of the Sámi hat is two-fold. The forerunner of the "four winds hat" was probably the eastern European cornered hat, which later became the four cornered hat of Sámi men. It most likely spread through the Pomor Trade between Russia and Norway along the Arctic Ocean coast. The South Sámi skull cap originated in southern Scandinavia in the Middle Ages. In the northern parts of Sweden the men's hat changed to

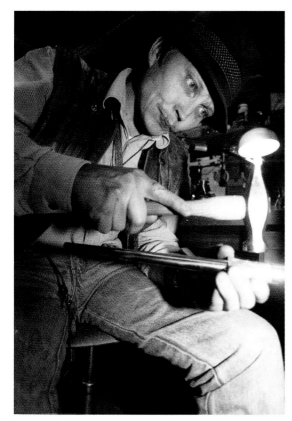

Petteri Laiti is an example of a Sámi handicraft artist who has succeeded through his own skills as well as through traditions and schooling. To the right a *solju* made by him and to the left he shapes a silver spoon. Photos: Jaakko Heikkilä and Petteri Laiti. The *Sámi Duodji* trademark guarantees the authenticity of Sámi handicraft.

have a visor and pompom; the women's was more like a bonnet.

Textiles were traditionally the realm of women. Summer clothing was made of cloth, while winter clothing was basically leather and fur. After World War II European styles of clothing became widespread among Sámi. Although most of the old styles have disappeared there has, nevertheless, been a return in some degree to the former garment styles. It has become more common to decorate the garments, and styles changed more rapidly in the 20th century, especially after the garments began to be used more and more as formal dress for festive occasions.

Traditionally hand work was made for daily needs and home use. The exception were specialized handicrafters such as boat and reindeer sled builders, who were able to sell their creations. Today, except for clothing, handicrafts are no longer primarily made for one's own use, but rather for sale. A result is that the border between handicraft and art handicraft is somewhat blurred.

True art handicrafters, of whom there are many, especially on the Swedish side of Sápmi, are of many opinions when drawing comparisons to professional artists. They use delicate designs to fashion traditional patterns. They make items for sale or exhibit; works that are valued for their aesthetic qualities are often bought by people outside the Sámi community. Many handicrafters are members of the *Sámi Daidda̧čehpiid Searvi* (Association of Sámi Artists).

115

SÁMI PICTORIAL ARTS

Sámi heritage of pictorial art reaches back to the rock drawings of thousands of years ago. Despite that modern day Sámi art takes its main influences from the ideals of western art, which became familiar through the schools and the world-view transmitted by the majority society. As in other arts, in Sámi pictorial art many of the most interesting works were born out of the interpretation of this contrast between the Sámi and Western worlds.

The relations of today's artists to the ancient heritage are problematic. It is natural that traditional symbolism and imagery take on central role in the works of pictorial artists. However, artists only indirectly assimilated these, because Sámi spiritual cultural traditions and history underwent a great change in the 1600s and 1700s in connection with Christian missionizing. The symbolism of the ancient rock art and noaidi drums has largely vanished, and the whole of the past world-view is difficult to sort out from the sources that were all written by outsiders. Not even a simple noaidi drum was preserved in Sápmi. Today, the few Sámi drums presented in exhibitions in Sápmi are on loan from European museums.

Iver Jåks and Nils-Aslak Valkeapää penetrated the rock images and ancient world-view through their books and photographs. Like other artists, they were not able, nor did they want to make use of the original meanings of the ancient symbols. Even so they are remarkable sources of inspiration that originated in the same environment and among the same people as today's art.

The heritage of traditional handicrafts, duodji, is the nearest aesthetic point of reference for artists. For example, Rose-Marie Huuva made duodji for a long time before she moved into western art forms and abstract expressions. The presence of the traditional work with wood, bone, roots and reindeer leather is seen in the works and world of design of many sculptors. The Sámi sense of colour is reflected in paintings and in the textile art of Britta Marakatt-Labba, for one.

Art handicraft forms a certain bond, almost a transitional form, between duodji and contemporary art. Like duodji, art handicraft is based on traditional materials and patterns, but may be somewhat modified. The main point of contact with contemporary art is that art handicraft has clearly diverged from daily use. It has become a commercial item whose main users are buyers outside the community. To them it is expressively the aesthetic scope of the item that is central.

The third line of tradition leads to the Sámi artists of the early 1900s, the pioneers of contemporary art. Only in the realm of general literary culture connected to Sápmi did Sámi pictorial artists' names become noticed. Pioneers of Sámi art Johan Turi and Nils Nilsson Skum became known through their books. Like the artists who made the rock drawings they wrote and drew to preserve knowledge, to transmit the age-old heritage to future generations.

Their's was the typical popular way of combining history, mythology and their own life story. It is important to note that for them making pictures and writing were not separate genres as they are for western artists and writers; the ancestral comprehensive concept of art can be seen in the integration of image in a text or narrative. Because of the documentary aspect their works were at least as much practical as aesthetic.

Johan Turi was folk art's idealistic representative; a man from Čohkkiras, who had never attend school, from a Reindeer Sámi family, who nevertheless gradually lost all his reindeer and started living in a Bohemian style. In his work *Muitalus sámiid birra* (1910; The Story of the Sámi) he ambitiously tried to paint a comprehensive picture of Sámi culture with all its immensity. Stylistically delicious in his use of language, Turi draws a naively characterized image, which also tried to depict a comprehensive picture of his subject.

Turi's depiction is so much related to the ancestral art of painting on rocks and noaidi drums that it is said to be connected, in its inheritance from the Stone Age, into a "continuum". However, he did not know of that heritage. A characteristic of Turi's drawings is the lack of a central perspective, but precisely through that and through images combining various realms of life he achieves an authentic feel of life, humming with action and events.

Skum, who was from Girjjis, had also left reindeer herding, had not been to school, and was picture maker and traditional narrator. He made his breakthrough in his later years, above all with his book *Same sita - Sameby* (Sámi Siida, 1938); his international exhibits in the 1930s also drew attention. Images of reindeer and nature were Skum's specialty; he had the ability to create powerful, complete pictures of wintry wilderness. Reindeer herding flowed so strongly in his veins that he is said to have priced his paintings on the basis of the number of reindeer in them.

The third outstanding pioneering Sámi artist was John Savio, from Mátta-Várjjat, who, unlike Turi and Skum, studied art. He attended the Oslo arts and crafts school in the 1920s. Before his premature death at 36 years of age he had made a name for himself for his woodcuts, which are favourites for illustrations in Sámi books still today.

The heritage of the self-taught Turi and Skum and the professionally trained Savio combined in an interesting way in two of the most prominent initiators of contemporary Sámi art: Lars Pirak from Johkamohkki and Iver Jåks from Kárášjohka, both born in 1932. They are both ex officio and honourary members of the *Sámi Dáiddačehpiid Searvi*. Both have mounted dozens of exhibits of their own works in the Nordic countries and have participated in exhibits throughout Europe, North America and Australia.

Especially characteristic was the beginning of Jåks' career. He was supposed to become a reindeer herder, but after an accident as a child on a reindeer sled ride he was in the hospital for many years. After attending art school in the South he returned to the North as an art teacher and became a full time artist in the 1960s. He shocked both his compatriots and the Norwegian public with his graphic works containing strong stands, such as his *Homo sapiens* series, which presents both political and sexual themes.

In his sculptures he wanted to bring out the ancient mythology; he gave it an extensive, abstract significance in his works. The best known of his trailblazing sculptures, and the largest, is *Veahčir* (Noaidi Drumstick), a seven metre tall monument located in Kárášjohka. His abstract sculptures are often mentioned for the incorporation of ideas of Sámi mythology.

Rock paintings in Bossegohppi at the Áltá Fjord. Photo: Pekka Sammallahti, 1988.

The veteran of Sámi art, Iver Jåks, uses traditional materials, but the language of abstract design. Photo: Marja Helander.

117

Mythology and present day in art

Iver Jåks is the most prominent trailblazer for Sámi modern art. His true breakthrough came about at the end of the 1970s through the advance of young artists born during and after the war. The most notable event was the formation of the *Sámi Dáiddárjoavku* (Sámi Art Group), also called the Máze Group, in 1978. In the group, which held extraordinary exhibits during the next five years, were its initiator Synnøve Persen, as well as Aage Gaup, Rannveig Persen, Josef Halse, Trygve Lund Guttormsen, Hans Ragnar Mathisen and Berit Marit Haetta.

Sámi Dáiddačehpiid Searvi (SDS) was founded the following year, in 1979, with active support of the Máze Group and Nils-Aslak Valkeapää. It drew together artists from all over Sápmi, organizing exhibits and directing activities through the *Sámi Daiddaguovddáš* (Sámi Art Centre), which was established in Kárášjohka in 1986. In 1980, the important Nordic project *Arts from the Arctic* exhibited the works of aboriginal artists from the whole circumpolar region.

Today's group of Sámi artists is large; in 1993 SDS had 44 members. Their techniques span nearly all sectors of modern art. The group includes sculptors, handicrafters, landscape painters, graphic artists, abstract artists and photographic artists. They come from all over Sápmi, from Mátta-Várjjat and North Cape to Southern Sápmi, and outside as far as Berlin.

Art production can often be triggered by a trauma that highlights the conflict between a person's background and new influences. Sometimes it is a concrete, physical trauma, such as Jåks' or Hans Ragnar Mathisen's. Mathisen, like Jåks, spent years of his childhood in hospital with tuberculosis that was raging in his home community. For the boy from Deatnu life in a hospital in the strange town of Romsa (Tromsa) left life long traumas which he dissolved by making art.

Sometimes the trauma may be more emotional as for Merja Aletta Ranttila. The torment of the religious experiences of her childhood and the painfully endured time at boarding schools away from her home environment spurred her to express herself through pictures. A more recent trauma, which brought with it a strengthening and even recognition of her Sámi identity, was the Álttá Conflict over a hydro-electric power plant at the beginning of the 1980s. Many artists, including the Máze Group as well as Britta Marakatt-Labba and Ingunn Utsi, took part in the confrontation at Stilla and experienced the Conflict as important, but terrible.

"I am from a small Sámi village, but I received a western art education. I have tried to fit these points of departure together without hurting myself." said Synnøve Persen. The issue was more than just differences in thought or in place. The artists had to find a balance between their childhood backgrounds and the present. As artists they were searching for their own voice in some middle ground between making pictures "naturally' or as they had been taught. By heritage they were Sámi, but their education and artistic training had been in institutes and conditions set up by the national majority populations.

Their works show the mutual influences of heritage and new impressions. Traditional Sámi imagery and pigments are most clearly seen in the works of Nils-Aslak Valkeapää and Hans Ragnar Mathisen. Valkeapää developed noaidi drum figures into new forms in his paintings and book illustrations. Mathisen became known primarily for his representation of the Sámi world-view in maps on which the place names, pictures and concepts of the earth are according to the Sámi spirit; Sápmi is at the centre of his "living map of the world'. Neither of these artists had had a connection to the symbols of noaidi drums passed down through their heritage. They felt a spiritual bond with the imagery of their forefathers, and they interpreted those images through modern views and experiences. Valkeapää said, "The ancient Sámi imagery is a language of its own in which many meanings can be found. It may be followed as its own story. Relived once more as living life and living nature, the ancient symbols must be read in a new light as new artistic expression; they create a dual illumination that takes on a new meaning."

Artists who are transforming traditions are also those handicrafters and art handicrafters who have gone on to develop their crafts in more artistic and

Aage Gaup from Kárášjohka is a carver who uses driftwood from the Arctic Ocean coast as material among other things. Photo: Jaakko Heikkilä.

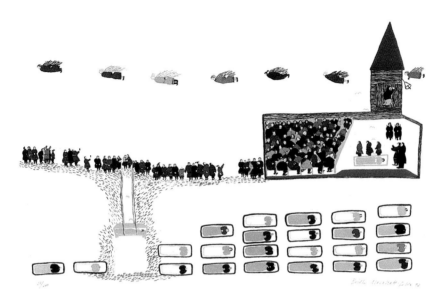

Britta Marakatt-Labba from Sohppar often displays humorous themes in her textile works. Her painting *The Journey* pictures Sámi mental concepts. Photo: Marja Helander.

symbolic directions. One example is Mailis Skaltje, from the Swedish side. She learned the skill of making leather clothing from her mother and uses traditional symbols. Nevertheless, she is also attraced by the way of making art that she was formally taught, conceptual art. In her work she has made studies of rounded and oval shaped "Sáminess" and contrasting "western" rectangular shapes.

On the other hand, there are artists who have evidently consciously broken away from romantic and exotic attempts with ancient symbolism and have instead brought forth new images (for example, Merja Aletta Ranttila), associated the old with humour and irony (Britta Marakatt-Labba), or concentrated on colour composition and feelings created in shades and tones (Synnøve Persen). Still, a distinct feature of modern day Sámi art is the connectedness of people and nature, just as it had been traditionally.

Beyond the natural feel, there is clearly an awareness of the new in their works. In the abstract graphic background of the works by Eva Aira, a Sámi from the Swedish side living in Kárášjohka, the vast northern landscape can be discerned.

Sissel Sofie Zahl from Várjjat bases her work on nature, but relationships between people interest her even more.

Some have shown the contrast between new and old by taking a startling stand, or through soft colours and a light touch. Persen's works are examples containing both sadness and aggression. Some of her subjects are experiences from a trip to Greenland, but the colours are from certain memories of childhood, "My childhood has coloured me", says the artist.

From Sohppar, Britta Marakatt-Labba's connection with tradition is clear, but it is not expressed through the choice of materials or techniques, but rather through her vision and ideas. Her textile works are often strongly inspired by mythology and tradition. In them she embodies traditional Sámi landscape but links it, often humorously, to the present day and to conflicting elements. A result of the Chernobyl nuclear power plant disaster, which desperately affected reindeer herding, especially on the Swedish side of Sápmi, was that her works were printed as postcards and her textile works in the colour of the Sámi garments were used on postage stamps. They were originally cries

120

of distress, set in art, on behalf of Sámi culture to the authorities.

Merja Aletta Ranttila is reminiscent of Marakatt-Labba, both in the tendency to react to current events and in her ironic outlook. The Chernobyl environmental catastrophe and the Persian Gulf war shocked Ranttila so much that she unburdened her anguish in a series of pictures. But she expands the imagery to humankind's wretchedness and despair in general, as in the work *Wounded Angel.*

Ranttila's work is divided, by her own definition, into night and day. The day pictures are postcards and book illustrations in soft tones, in which she presents traditional Sámi themes. They form the economic base for her work as an artist. The night pictures are sombre black woodcuts in which she releases her own inner torment. The depressing aspect is lightened by her original, cheerful style.

Among the other artists on the Finnish side of Sápmi, Seija Ranttila, in her modern design, makes use of patterns from Finnish art of the 1960s as well as traditional Sámi colours and patterns. Her work has been called "modern ethnic" textile art. The graphicist Liisa Helander is especially well-known as a book illustrator, and her cover designs and drawings have been shown in many exhibits. Writer Kerttu Vuolab is also well-known as an illustrator of her own books, such as *Ánde ja Risten jagi fárus.*

The themes used by Sea Sámi Ingunn Utsi are very closely linked to her childhood and appear to her as ideal contrasts to her time at school in Norwegian surroundings. Her figure of a bird is a kind of self-portrait through which she examines her own traumas and feelings. Utsi uses traditional materials like wood and stone in her sculptures, and modern plexiglass as well. For her, plexiglass is a natural material that can also take her back to her childhood. It evokes the window of her childhood home; through its broken pane the child's view of the world always looked different.

Utsi, as a sculptor, is a typical Sámi artist. Many Sámi followed in the footsteps of Iver Jåks, becoming sculptors. Sculpting seems to be natural because it uses traditional materials. The starting point of relief sculptor Aage Gaup is an attempt to integrate the Sámi perception and the modern sense of form, space and materials.

Elly Mathilde Johnsen, a sculptor from Várjjat, has made installations using quite special materials, primarily stones used and revered by her ancestors. Annelise Josefsen, born in Hammerfest, uses traditional materials in combination with different types of glass. She blends traditional motifs, such as stylized arrows, as leading themes for her abstract sculptures.

Rose Marie Huuva, along with Gaup, is the most well-known Sámi sculptor in the world. Huuva comes from a Sámi village near Giron on the Swedish side. She grew up doing Sámi handicrafts as a family tradition. She also studied handicrafts and, in the 1970s, she clearly dedicated herself to that field. From modern design for clothing and textiles she turned more and more to sculpture, which she also used in her textile works. Through that she dug deeper into the world of symbols and abstract forms. The symbolic feel is strong in her descriptive sculpture of a creature halted in its growth, mummy-like.

Sámi photographic art began to develop at the end of the 1970s with works by Niillas A. Somby, from Sirbmá at the Deatnu. He made a statement with pictures of the changes in Sámi life, as did Harry Johansen in the 1980s. Somby actively participated in the Álttá Conflict, where the public picture of Sámi was formed through the challenging photos published in the paper *Sámi Áigi.* The artistic direction of Sámi photography was developed by such people as Ivar Murberg, Bente Gaving and the younger, gifted multi-media artists Lena Stenberg (from the Swedish side) and Marja Helander (from the Finnish side) whose "identity trips" went from European metropolises to the Ohcejohka countryside.

Merja Aletta Ranttila from Aanaar experienced the wrath of ministers for "depicting the devil" at the "Shaman Summer" happening in Tornio in 1992.

For Ingunn Utsi from Porsáŋgu, plexiglass is the natural material at the edge of tradition. Photo: Marja Helander, 1995.

Textile artist Seija Ranttila is a big name in "ethnodesign". Photo: Jorma Lehtola, 1995.

THEATRE AND FILM

Sámi theatre is a prime example of how a new language of art is born out of contemporary impulses and needs. Sámi never really had true theatre, apart from certain rituals. Nonetheless, theatre has become possibly the most distinctive of Sámi art forms. The *Beaivváš* theatre stages several productions each year and has considerably strengthened Sámi identity by bringing performances to the smallest places all over Sápmi.

Beaivváš was born during the Álta Conflict when it performed all over the Nordic countries taking a stand against the damming of the river with the musical *Min duoddarat* (Our Fells). The theatre company draws its inspiration from Sámi heritage and narrative tradition, and also from world literature and aboriginal theatre around the globe. *Beaivváš'* dramatizations have told of stállu (the giant spirit) and *čuđit* (legendary ruthless and violent enemies) and have reflected on Sámi history. It has also presented modern plays such as a version of Frederico García Lorca's *Varra heajat* (Bodas de sangre, 1933; Blood Wedding), in which the wedding banquet consisted, naturally, of dried meat and yoik was performed along with flamenco.

Beaivváš has told many kinds of stories from ancient history to present day. *Sámi Prinsa* (The Sámi Prince) tells the true tale of a Sámi fraud who travelled to the courts of Europe passing himself off as royalty. The war years and their impact have also been the subject of several plays. *Beaivváš* has also presented performances for youth, such as the rock musical *Earalágan* (Different), and children's plays that deal with issues like school bullying, in addition to fairy tales.

Of course, *Beaivváš* is not the only Sámi way to produce theatre. The *Dálvadis* theatre company, on the Swedish side, takes inspiration as much from European dance theatre as it does from aboriginal peoples' performances using mime and mythology. One of their members, Åsa Simma, joined with Norman Charles, an Iroquois, to form the two person theatre troop *Hiwak*, which combines Sámi and Indian heritage in its pieces.

At the Deatnu, on the Finnish side, the inspiring amateur theatre company *Rávgoš* has performed as a folk theatre creating appealing performances for a general public by dealing with local events and every day experiences and adventures. Founded in Vuovdaguoika in 1981, *Rávgoš* repertory has extended from comedy to powerful productions incorporating sensitive issues, such as the mentally ill.

Film is the newest area of Sámi art. Sámi have been the subject of countless films beginning in the 1910s, but always as seen from an outsider's viewpoint. They have been portrayed in documentaries stressing the search for the "genuine" Sámi. Almost every documentary pictures reindeer herders' life and harmonious relation with nature, never ever any modern influences.

In Sámi films the documentary and fiction genres have been kept, but they have taken on completely new dimensions. The year 1987 may be taken as the birth year of Sámi fiction film, with the premier of Nils Gaup's first movie *Ofelaš* (The Pathfinder). It is based on an old Sámi tale of *čuđit*, enemies whose violent deeds in Sápmi are stopped by the cunning of the main character.

The critical agent is Nature, from which the enemies have become estranged in a disastrous way; in the film they do not even use skis. Besides being fast moving and lively, the film is strongly symbolic in its use of the folk tale style to distinguish "us" from "the others". This is shown by the use of language: the Sámi language on screen, lively, for the first time. The enemy's language is deliberately clumsy gibberish, not more than demanding cries. The actors were mainly from the *Beaivvaš* theatre. In his later films Gaup did not use Sámi themes until he began to plan a film about the 1852 Guovdageaidnu Uprising.

Another prominent director is Paul-Anders Simma, a Sámi from the Swedish side. He began his career with a film about trapping ptarmigan *Dobbelis ija ja beaivvi* (1987; Beyond Night and Day). The conflict between the new and the old is examined through the relationship of a grandfather living amidst nature and his young grandson living in the city. Simma's outlook is optimistic - the boy learns to understand the values of the old way of life in nature.

Simma's breakthrough, the short film *Let's Dance* (1991), is the humorous story of a boy's first trip to a dance. The shy boy's feelings of love change to joyful infatuation after using snuff one

Performer and musician Sverre Porsanger (above) has been a leading name in the *Beaivvaš* Theatre. He also acted in the film *Ofelaš* (The Pathfinder) which was nominated for the best foreign produced film of the year for the Oscar awards in 1987 (below). Photo: Jorma Lehtola.

night; this also brings a jolly band of black musicians and a talking reindeer to the lonely village winter road. *Guovža* (1994; The Bear) is a mythical film based on a Skolt Sámi tale. It portrays a girl's love for a man who has the form of a bear, and their son's oedipal relationship to his parents.

In addition to films of pure fiction Simma has distinguished himself with his documentary work on the traditional portrayal of Sámi. His subjects and ideas are not those of anthropologists. *Vaši eatnamat* (1993; Lands of Hate) tells of the conflict between city people and Reindeer Sámi in Hammerfest, where reindeer wandering from their summer pastures come into the streets and flower gardens to graze.

The feature length film *Duoddara árbi* (1995; Fell's Testament) probes deeply into the main conflicts among reindeer herders, above all the taboo of reindeer theft. Competition over dwindling pasture lands has torn apart Sámi solidarity, and is experienced by Junna, the film's youngest reindeer herder. While the State is trying to persuade him to quit reindeer herding by offering money for slaughtering his herd, the reindeer owners of larger

Paul Anders Simma (above) has produced documentaries and fiction movies, such as *Sagojoga Minister* in 1997 (right). Photos: Jorma Lehtola. Skábmagovat is an aboriginal people´s film festival held in Aanaar every January (below).

herds are forcing the smaller herders off the pastures. Modern times offer Junna a solution; by supplying 30 sled reindeer for the Lillehammar Winter Olympics he can continue his father's tradition, at least for a time.

As a counterbalance to his sombre films, Simma made *Beatnaga eallin* (1995; A Dog's Life) a humorous film about the old age of a Parisian dog and a reindeer dog. The *Ministtar* (1997; The Minister of State) is a rascal comedy that takes place at the crossroads of many cultures and nationalities at the shores of the Arctic Ocean during the war. It is a farce about the absurdity of war and the mishaps among people's relationships caused by its unusual conditions.

In addition to Simma, there are many other documentary film makers in Sápmi who have made movies for TV on important issues. One of the most important has been Johns Kalvemo, the television producer for the Kárášjohka Sámi Radio. In the 1970s he made a unique documentary of the situation of the Kola Sámi society which at that time was closed. Later Kalvemo documented how the skulls that had been taken from Sápmi were returned. He also retraced the journey that the testers for the French car maker Citroën made in the 1930s testing the new model.

In recent years, especially on the Norwegian side, in-

vestment has begun to be made in the production of Sámi language programmes for children and young people. The young people's series *Skáidi* (1996), like Simma's film, dealt with reindeer theft, but also delved into personal relationships of youth and the adventures of the Arctic rowing team. Rauna Paadar-Leivo's screenplay *Káre Nina* (1997) for a TV series aimed at the very young is about children's friendship with a mysterious girl of the forest who has supernatural powers.

The main forum for Sámi movie and TV production has been the aboriginal peoples' film festival *Skábmagovat* (Reflections of Endless Night) held annually in Aanaar. Since 1999 the event, held in the cold of mid winter, has presented the productions of Sámi as well as other aboriginal peoples, such as Aboriginees, Inuit, and Brazilian Indians.

Nils-Aslak Valkeapää put the tradition of the Sámi people into words. Photo: Jaakko Heikkilä.

NILS-ASLAK VALKEAPÄÄ'S TWO LIVES

Áilloháš or Áilu, Nils-Aslak Valkeapää, lived two lives. The first began in March 1943 during the war when he was born into a Reindeer Sámi family in Eanodat municipality. The family was living in their winter home in Ádjagorsa in Gáresávvon. It was just before their spring migration to the coast of Norway at Ivguvuotna or Ivgubahta.

The family later moved their winter home to Beattet, which was also Áilu's winter home for the whole of his first life. He spent the summers in Ivgu. In his own way Áilu followed the ancient Reindeer Sámi annual migration his whole life long. Personally, and as an artist, he was truly a "migrating Sámi", whose wanderings reached different areas of art and the edges of the world.

At the end of February 1996 Valkeapää was in a violent car accident near his home in Beattet, when, in a snow flurry, he collided with a semi-trailer on the road to Gilbbesjávri.

He woke up to masses of flowers and thought he was in heaven. But he really did start a new life. The world was to him as to a newborn baby. He did not remember how a television or computer worked. He lost his foreign languages; some, like Norwegian, returned, but English never did.

After returning home from the hospital he picked up a letter in the mail requesting him to read the included manuscript. He read it and liked the text very much   but who could have written it? He had also forgotten that a book manuscript was sent back to the author before its publication.

Áilu adjusted to his new condition amazingly well. He said, "I am an instrument that life plays". Because of his health he had to move from Beattet to Ivgubahta, where he was very much appreciated. The municipality and the Norwegian government helped him to build a grand studio house, *Lassa Gammi* (Stone Gammi), perched above the shores of the beautiful Ivguvuotna.

His second life ended on his good friend's sofa in Espoo, Finland, after returning from a trip to Japan. Áilu died in a manner worthy of the son of a Reindeer Sámi and of a poet: *jodus*, on the move.

Borders

Valkeapää was born into a mode of living that crossed the borders of nations and cultures.

"I came from a multicultural community and I still live in three countries." he said. "We never paid attention to borders, and I never even knew that there were different countries until I went to school."

The young Áilloháš concisely summed up the issue in a provocative book *Terveisiä Lapista* (1971, Greetings from Lapland, 1983):

"I was born in Bálojotnjálbmi in Eanodat, soon, during the evacuation, I got to know the hardships of the world in the fells on the Swedish side. My mother is a Sámi from the Norwegian side. My father's relatives are far away on the Swedish side, at least as far away as the Arctic Circle. I live by the side of the border zone, at least when I happen to live there."

"When I went to elementary school I found out that I did not have a mother tongue. [...]"

"Today when I am at home in Beattet I notice that I do not have a fatherland."

Perhaps that is the origin of Valkeapää's ability to cross cultural and political borders as well as the borders of art. From the intersection of many cultures, he looked at things freely, without borders. He naturally was busy in many international activities, travelling the world as the Sámi's "ambassador". In his view he was not acting internationally. It was only his natural way to communicate.

In the same way all art forms met and crossed in Valkeapää's artworks. He was a poet, writer, yoiker, musician, composer, photographer, painter, pictorial artist, cultural politician and performer. The different forms blended together: yoik melted into jazz, music into Sámi language, visual art into literature.

The artist himself said, "The essential for a Sámi artist has always been that they work in many areas of art. Earlier the reason was that you had to be able to do almost everything. Now the reason is more prosaic; in Sápmi you can't make a living from just one art form."

Strange fish

In Nils-Aslak Valkeapää's epic poem *Beaivi, Áhčážan* the first picture a person sees is the full moon seen through a tent's smoke hole. The person who sees it becomes an exceptional person, an artist and maker of pictures, who sees in the way of a noaidi. That person draws away from everything, only observing, creating. The main character, looking aside at possessions, accompanies and lives life with them.

The memory of the moon was Valkeapää's own. He was the only boy in a Reindeer Sámi family, and he found his playmates among the birds and plants of Ádjagorsa. Everything new awakened his imaginations. "When a lone child sees a track in the fells he happily follows it," he said.

Áilu got his language and traditional way of life from his home and his view of the world from Nature. From childhood he soaked up inspirations from western culture, too. Already at the age of four he went to the itinerant catechist school in a neighbour's house. Instead of the lessons, he remembered only his own wildly flying thoughts. On school days he usually sat under the table looking at the patterns made by the grain of the wood on the underside of the table. They opened another world where he followed amazing tales and adventures.

Those two weeks were the only schooling for his sisters, but Áillohaš was allowed to continue in the elementary school. He had to move into the boarding house in Gáresávvon, away from home. In a later poem Valkeapää described the school surroundings as a place where time is different, the days longer, the language foreign, and "feeling suddenly like fishing / secretly sneaking to the small pond / and hook small red-eyed strange fish."

The strange fish were roach, which the boys fished with hooks stuck into pieces of dough. Roach did not reach north as far as Beattet, but only to Gáresávvon. Áilu himself felt like a strange fish, not only among other children, but among adults, too. He was a dreamer, a bookworm. All the books in the library were not enough for him.

Even in Beattet he was different. As reindeerman Johannes Valkeapää commented on his son's killing of a reindeer, "That wont do". It was upsetting for the boy as well. His father did not scold him then or ever, but perhaps he already understood that the child's path would lead to a very different way than that of their forefathers.

Áilu's path led to the Anár Christian folk high school and from there to the teachers seminary in Kemijärvi, where he finished the middle school courses in two years. Áilu became a teacher, but never followed a teaching career.

More than just dull studies, the time he spent in the teachers seminary had a cultural and spiritual impact. He found an echo to his own ideas of what it means to be Sámi from other young people. Together they were responsible for the radical methods used from the 1960s onward to raise up the Sámi culture.

The Sámi ambassador

Valkeapää was the most prominent proponent of the "Sámi renaissance", which began at the end of the 1960s. Through his appearances and concerts he brought back value and dignity to the despised and rejected yoik tradition and revived its popularity with youth. His classic record *Joikuja* (1968) was the first modern day recording of Sámi music. He dashed the myths about Sámi in a polemic and mettlesome book *Terveisiä Lapista* (Greetings from Lapland, 1971).

With his collections of poetry he took a lyrical stand in the Sámi's search for self-esteem in the 1970s. He took Sámi music in new directions, combining yoik and western musical forms, even the symphony. In his paintings and photography

After a severe car accident in late winter 1996, Nils-Aslak Valkeapää took up permanent residence in Ivgubahta at the shore of the ocean which always meant much to him and his family and relatives. On the back cover of his 1974 record *Vuoi, Biret-Maaret, vuoi!* he included a self-portrait. He died unexpectedly in November 2001.

131

Valkeapää showed paths toward new directions.

As a writer his most important gifts to Sámi culture were the large works of poetry *Ruoktu vaimmus* (1985), *Beaivi, Áhčážan* (1988) and *Eanni, eannázan* (2001). Based on those works, he has deservedly been called the Sámi people's mythographer and interpreter of their national mythology and identity.

He gradually grew to be a symbolic personage for Sámi themselves and in the eyes of outsiders. In the early 1970s he was "Finland's Áilu" in Guovdageaidnu and on the Swedish side "Válgon Áilu". But toward the end of his life he was to all the Sámi only Áilu, Áillohaš.

Writing and print making were just as natural to Áilu as music. He said that he does not remember a time when he did not do them. It was just as natural for him to combine different forms, from literature to print making, from music to poetry. He saw nothing strange in that. The natural life was for him unlimited.

"When I paint, I hear it as music and words; when I make music, I see it as colours and words; when I write, music is in my head the whole time and I see colours. Different art forms are products of the same spirit, only carried out with different techniques. Crossing borders and forms has always seemed natural for me. What seems strange is someone who only writes or only draws."

One man, the whole nation

Holistic integrity was Valkeapää's essential characteristic. In his epic poems his conscious ambition was to create a comprehensive picture of the Sámi people, their world of thought and their traditions. While *Ruoktu váimmus* was the first psychological accounting, *Beaivi, Áhčážan* was plainly a conscious effort to create an "epic of the Sámi people", which would have symphonic dimensions in its structure. The photographs are an integral part of the tale.

As is appropriate for an epic, *Beaivi, Áhčážan* begins with the creation of the world, "the embryo of life in the womb of the world". Humanity appears gradually in the poetry; they make pictures on the rocks and on noaidi drumheads. Here the photographs are of rocks and shrines, flat rocks which vaguely resemble people.

Beaivi, Áhčážan is both the tale of one Sámi's life after the war and a portrayal of the whole world-view of the Sámi people. The main character is a Sámi who cannot kill a reindeer. Instead of living as others, he becomes a noaidi and an artist with his drums and the realities born out of them. In poetry and pictures, goahti, Sámi siidas, reindeer migration and markets all come to life.

But in the poem are the threatening shadows of strangers, conquerors, rulers who bring with them new boundaries, new goods, "they are fine / educated men / they could not sit at the fire". With the newcomers come new ideas and concepts, which have neither the adaptability of the northern residents nor their humility.

A quality that permeates the work is the Sámi concept of time. Just as a person's life, history also recurs as "seasons" - from birth to death, from morning to night, spring to winter and to a new spring, appearance to disappearance. *Beaivi, Áhčážan* is a great homage to Nature, the turning of the world, totally in harmony with the Sámi way of thinking. At the end of time, everything will melt again into the wholeness of the world, into dream.

In the poetry everything ends at the beginning. The book finally blends into a picture - he no longer knows whether he is real - or only his own picture. "I open the door to the outside / when I step inside". The work ends with photographs of rock drawings and sieidi, flat pictures, rocks that vaguely resemble people.

> *ja go visot lea meaddel*
> *ii gullo šat mihkkege*
> *ii mihkkege*
>
> *ja dat gullo*
>
>
> when all is finished
> nothing can be heard
> nothing
>
> and it is heard

(poem translated by Linna Weber Müller-Wille)

GLOSSARY OF PLACE NAMES

E = English, F = Finnish, N = Norwegian,
R = Russian, S = Swedish in parenthesis

Where several groups of Sámi overlap both names are used in the text, with the first being the most prominent in the area and the other in ()

Áŋŋel	Angeli (F)
Ádjagorsa	
Áltá, Alaheadju	Alta (N)
Ávži	
Ávjovárri	
Anár (Aanaar)	Inari (F)
Anár (Aanaarjávri)	Inarijärvi (F)
Anárjohka	Inarijoki (F)
Avvil (Avveel)	Ivalojoki (F)
Avvir	Imandra (R)
Báhaveadji	Paatsjoki (F)
Báhčaveadjijohka	
Bálojávri	Palojärvi (F)
Bálojotnjálbmi	Palojoensuu (F)
Beattet	Pättikkä (F)
Biton (Bihtán)	Piteå (S)
Bossogohppi	Bossekop (N)
Čáhcesuolu	Vadsø (N)
Če'vetjäu'rr (Čeavetjávri)	Sevettijärvi (F)
Čohkkiras	Jukkasjärvi (S, F)
Čovčjäävri	Syysjärvi (F)
Deatnu	Teno (F), Tana (N)
Divttasvuotna	Tysfjord (N)
Duortnus	Tornio (F), Torneå (S)
Eanodat	Enontekiö (F)
Gáddeluokta	Kandalakša (R)
Gáivuotna	Kåfjord (N)
Gápmas (Kaamas)	Kaamanen (F)
Gárasavvon	Kaaresuvanto (F), Karesuando (S)

Gáregasnjárga	Karigasniemi (F)
Geavŋŋis (Keeu'ŋes)	Boris Gleb (R), Skoltefossen (N), Kolttaköngäs (F)
Giehtaruohtas	Käsivarsi (F)
Giepma	Kemi (F)
Gihttel	Kittilä (F)
Giiggajávri	Kitkajärvi (F)
Gilbbesjávri	Kilpisjärvi (F)
Girjjis	Norrkaitum (S)
Giron	Kiruna (S)
Golmmešoaivi	Kolmmesoaivi (F), Golmisoaivve (N)
Guoládat	Kola (R)
Guoládatnjárga	Kolskij poluostrov (R), Kola Peninsula (E)
Guossan	Kuusamo (F)
Guovdageaidnu	Kautokeino (F, N)
Heahttá	Hetta (F)
Ivgu	Lyngen (N)
Ivgubahta	Skibotn (N)
Ivguvuotna	Lyngenfjord (N)
Jiellevárri	Gällivare (S)
Johkamohkki	Jokkmokk (N)
Kárášjohka	Karasjok (N)
Likšu	Lycksele (S)
Lohttu	Lutto (F)
Luja'vrr (Lujávri)	Lovozero (R)
Luleju	Luleå (S)
Málatvuotna	Malangen (N)
Másealgi	Maanselkä (F)
Mátta-Várjjat	Sør-Varanger (N)
Máze	Masi (N)
Njellim, Njeä'llem	Nellim (F)
Njauddâm (Njávdán)	Neiden (N), Näätämö (F)

Ohcejohka	Utsjoki (F)
Paaččjokk (Báhčaveadji)	Paatsjoki (F), Pasvikelv (N)
Peäccam (Beahcán)	Petsamo (F)
Peälbájävri	Pielpajärvi (F)
Porsáŋgu	Porsanger (N)
Romsa (Tromsa)	Tromsø (N)
Sállivárri	Sallivaara (F)
Sápmi	The Sámi homeland (E)
Sirbmá	Sirma (N)
Skiervá	Skjervøy (N)
Skillet	Skelefteå (S)
Soabbat	Sompio (F)
Soadegilli	Sodankylä (F)
Sohppar	Soppero (S)
Suo'nn'jel (Suonnjel)	Suonikylä (F)
Suorssá	Sorsele (S)
Troandin	Trondheim (N)
Ubmi	Umeå (S)
Umbajávri	Umbozero (R)
Umbbtek	Hiipinä (F)
	Gory Hibinskie Tundra (R)
Unjárga	Nesseby (N)
Várggát	Vardø (N)
Várjavuotna	Varangerfjorden (N)
Várjjat	Varanger (N)
Vuohčču	Vuotso (F)
Vuovdaguoika	Outakoski (F)

Siidas mentioned in text:

Másealgi	Maanselkä (F)
Giiggajávri	Kitkajärvi (F)
Čalmny-Varre	Ivanovka (R)
Arsjohka (Ar's'ëgk)	Arsjok (N)
	Varzino (R)
Suo'nn'jel (Suonnjel)	Suonikylä (F)
Muotki	Muotka (R)
Njauddâm (Njávdán)	Näätämö (F)
	Neiden (N)
Paaččjokk	Paatsjoki (F)
Áhkkil (Ä'kkel)	Akkala (F)
	Babinsk (R)
Deatnu	Tenonkylä (F)
	Tanaby (N)

Laplands mentioned:

Finnish Lapland
Kemi Lapland
Kola Lapland
Lule Lapland
Pite Lapland
Russian Lapland
Swedish-Finnish Lapland
Swedish Lapland
Torneå Lapland
Ume Lapland

LITERATURE BY AND ABOUT SÁMI

People, Culture, Language and Environment
Compiled by
Ludger Müller-Wille
(Department of Geography, McGill University, Montréal, Canada)

The following bibliography represents selected publications written by Sámi authors and other authors about Sámi in Latin, English, German and French. This list is not exhaustive, however, the range of publications was chosen to provide the interested reader with information on pertinent works that, in most cases, are easily accessible in libraries and bookstores in European and other countries. These publications deal mostly with culture, art, literature, socio-economic conditions, politics, landscape and environment. People with special interests and broader linguistic skills will find an extensive and rich literature in the Sámi languages, Finnish, Norwegian, Swedish, Russian as well as other languages in which works on Sámi have been published throughout the years. Cultural institutions - museums and bookstores - throughout Sápmi carry most of the publications which are still in print or are being released constantly.

Literature in Latin

(first ethnographical monograph about the Sámi and their land, Sápmi, which shaped the external image of the Sámi for a long time; this book became a bestseller in Europe through its rapid translations into English (1674), German (1675), French (1678) - see below - and other languages.

Schefferus, Joannis 1673. Lapponia. Frankfurt, Leipzig: Christian Wolff.

Literature in English

Sámi authors:

Aikio, Samuli & Ulla Aikio-Puoskari, Johannes Helander 1994. The Sami Culture in Finland. Helsinki: Lapin sivistysseura.

Báiki. The North American Sami Journal. Founded in 1991. The Saami Báiki Foundation. (http://www.baiki.org)

Gaski, Harald (ed.) 1996. In the Shadow of the Midnight Sun. Contemporary Sami Prose and Poetry. Kárášjohka: Davvi Girji.

Gaski, Harald (ed.) 1997. Sami Culture in a New Era. The Norwegian Sami Experience. Karasjok: Davvi Girji OS.

Hætta, Odd Mathis 1993. Sami - An Indigenous People of the Arctic. Karasjok: Davvi Girji.

Helander, Elina (ed.) 1996. Awakened Voices. The Return of Sami Knowledge. Guovdageaidnu/Kautokeino: Nordic Sami Institute.

Helander, Elina [and Kaarina Kailo] (eds.) 1998. No Beginning, No End. Sami Speak Up. Edmonton: Canadian Circumpolar Institute, University of Alberta.

[Pennanen, Jukka] and Klemetti Näkkäläjärvi (eds.) 2002. Siidastallan. From Lapp Communities to Modern Sámi Life. [Inari:] Sámi Museum Foundation.

Seurujärvi-Kari, Irja and Steinar Pedersen, Vuokko Hirvonen 1997. The Sámi. The Indigenous People of Northernmost Europe. Brussels: European Bureau of Lesser Used Languages.

Seurujärvi-Kari, Irja (coordinator) 2001ff. Saami Culture Encyclopedia. Helsinki: Sámi Studies,

Helsinki University. (http://www.helsinki.fi/saami/home.html)

[Siuruainen, Eino and] Pekka Aikio 1977. The Lapps in Finland - the population, their livelihood and their culture. Lapin Sivistysseuran julkaisuja 39. Helsinki: Lapin Sivistysseura.

Solbakk, Aage (ed.) 1990. The Sami People. Karasjok: Sámi Instituhtta & Davvi Girji O. S.

Turi, Johan 1910. Turi's Book of Lapland. Edited and translated into Danish by Emilie Demant Hatt. Translated from the Danish by E. Gee Nash. (Original title: Muittalus Samid Birra). New York & London: Harper & Brothers.

Valkeapää, Nils-Aslak 1983. Greetings from Lappland. The Sami - Europe's Forgotten People. Translated from the Norwegian by Beverley Wahl [Helsing frå sameland. Oslo: Pax Forlag, 1979; original Finnish: Terveisiä Lapista. Helsinki: Otava 1971]. London: Zed Press.

Valkeapää, Nils-Aslak 1994. Trekways of the Wind. Translated from the Sámi by Harald Gaski, Lars Nordström and Ralph Salisbury. (Original: Ruoktu váimmus. Guovdageaidnu: DAT 1985). Vaasa: DAT.

Valkeapää, Nils-Aslak 1997. The Sun, My Father. Translated from Sámi by Ralph Salisbury, Lars Nordström and Harald Gaski. (Original: Beaivi, Áhčážan. Vaasa: DAT 1988) Guovdageaidnu: DAT.

Other authors:

Beach, Hugh 1981. Reindeer Herding Management in Transition. The Case of Tuorpon Saameby in Northern Sweden. Stockholm: Almqvist & Wiksell International.

Beach, Hugh 1993. A Year in Lapland: Guest of the Reindeer Herders. Washington, DC: Smithsonian Institution.

Bosi, Roberto 1960. The Lapps. London & New York: Thames & Hudson, Praeger.

Dana, Kathleen Osgood 2003. Áillohaš the Shaman-Poet and his Govadas-Image Drum. A Literary Ecology. Acta Universitatis Ouluensis, Humanoria B 50. Oulu: University of Oulu.

Collinder, Björn 1949. The Lapps. New York: Americam-Scandinavian Society.

Eidheim, Harald 1971. Aspects of the Lappish Minority Situation. Oslo: Universitetsforlaget.

Ersson, Boris and Birgitta Hedin 1978. We are Lapps. Lapp Children Tell About Themselves. Oslo: Tiden Norsk Forlag.

Gourlie, Norah 1939. A Winter with Finnish Lapps. London: Blackie.

Ingold, Tim 1976. The Skolt Lapps Today. Cambridge: Cambridge University Press.

Jahreskog, Birgitta (ed.) 1982. The Sami National Minority in Sweden. Stockholm: Almqvist & Wiksell International.

Manker, Ernst 1953. Lapland and the Lapps. Stockholm: Nordisk Rotogravyr.

Manker, Ernst 1972. People of Eight Seasons. New York: Crescent Books.

Nickul, Karl 1977. The Lappish Nation. Citizens of Four Countries. Bloomington, Indiana: Indiana University.

Nuttal, Mark (ed.) 2004. Encyclopedia of the Arctic. London: Fitzroy Dearborn Publisher.

Paine, Robert 1957, 1965. Coast Lapp Society 1: A Study in Neighbourhood in Revsbotn Fjord (1957) & 2: A Study of Economic and Social Values (1965). Tromsø: Tromsø Museum.

Paine, Robert 1982. Dam a River, Damn a People? Saami (Lapp) Livelihood and the Alta/Kautokeino Hydro-Electric Project and the Norwegian Parliament. IWGIA Document 45. Copenhagen: IWGIA.

Paine, Robert 1994. Herds of the Tundra. A Portrait of Saami Reindeer Pastoralism. Washington, DC: Smithsonian Institution.

Pelto, Pertti J. 1962. Individualism in Skolt Lapp Society. Helsinki: [National Museum].

Pelto, Pertti J. 1973. The Snowmobile Revolution: Technology and Social Change in the Arctic. Menlo Park, CA: Cummings (reissued: Prospect Heights, IL: Waveland Press 1987.)

Robinson, Michael and Karim-Aly Kassam 1998. Sami Potato. Living with Reindeer and Perestroika. Calgary: Bayeux Arts Inc.

Sammallahti, Pekka 1998. The Saami Languages. An Introduction. Kárášjohka: Davvi Girji.

Scheffer, Johannes 1674. The History of Lapland. Oxford. (facsimile reprint: Suecia rediviva 22. Stockholm 1971.)

Spencer, Arthur 1978. The Lapps. New York: Crane, Russak & Company Inc., Newton Abbot: David & Charles.

Svensson, Tom G 1997. The Sami and Their Land. Oslo: Novus forlag.

Vitebsky, Piers 1993. Saami of Lapland - Threatened Cultures. New York: Thomson Learning. (aimed at children)

Literatur auf Deutsch

Sámische AutorInnen:

Haetta, Odd Mathis 1995. Die Sámit. Ureinwohner der Arktis. Übersetzt von Christina Schafranek, bearbeitet von Birgit Kretschmann, Revision der Übersetzung Klaus Peter Nickel. Karasjok: Davvi Girji o.s.

Paltto, Kirsti 1997. Zeichen der Zerstörung. Übersetzung aus dem Finnischen von Regine Pirschel. (Original: Gurzo luotta (sámisch). Ohcejohka:

Gielas, 1991; Juokse nyt naalin poika (finnisch). Oulu: Pohjoinen, 1993) Mannheim: Persona Verlag.

Turi, Johan 1912. Das Buch des Lappen Johan Turi. Erzählungen von dem Leben der Lappen. Hsg. von Emilie Demant Hatt. Frankfurt: Rütten & Loening. [Originalfassung auf Sámisch und Dänisch: Turi, Johan 1910. Muittalus Samid Birra. København: Graebers boktrykkeri.]

Valkeapää, Nils-Aslak 1985. Ich bin des windigen Berges Kind. Lieder und Texte aus Lappland. Übersetzung von H. U. Schwaar. Wald: Verlag Im Waldgut.

Andere AutorInnen:

Bernatzik, Hugo Adolf 1935. Lappland. Leipzig: Verlag Bibliographisches Institut.

Crottet, Robert 1955. Verzauberte Wälder. Legenden aus Lappland. Hamburg: Christian Wegner Verlag.

Crottet, Robert 1963. Nordlicht. Geschichten und Legenden aus Lappland. Hamburg: Christian Wegner Verlag.

Crottet, Robert 1966 [1980]. Am Rande der Tundra. Reise durch Lappland. Hamburg: Wegner Verlag [Frankfurt: Fischer Taschenbuch Verlag.]

Crottet, Robert und Enrique Méndez 1968. Lappland. Hamburg: Christian Wegner Verlag.

Fromm, Hans (Hsg.) 1978. Aufsätze / Berichte / Erzählung / Dichtung Mitteilungen aus der Deutschen Bibliothek, Jahrbuch für finnisch-deutsche Literaturbeziehungen 12. Helsinki / Helsingfors: Deutsche Bibliothek.
Mit Beiträgen und Gedichten von sámischen AutorInnen: Samuli Aikio, Johan Turi, Paulus Utsi, Nils Mathis Vars, Kirsti Paltto und Nils-Aslak Valkeapää.

Gardi, René 1939. Puoris Päivä! Im Flußboot and zu Fuß durch Finnisch Lappland. Bern, Leipzig: P. Haupt.

Guting, Katharina 1991. Rivgu. Zur Marginalisierung der Frau in der samischen Rentierzüchterbevölkerung Schwedens. Bonn: Holos Verlag. (Dissertation, Ethnologie, Bonn)

Hagemann, Gustav 1976. Das Leben der Lappen in ihren Ritzungen und anderen Zeugnissen. Iserlohn: Sauerland-Verlag.

Hein, Manfred Peter (Hsg.) 1985. Beiträge zur finnischen, finnlandschwedischen, lappischen, estnischen, lettischen und litauischen Literatur. Traject 5/1985. Stuttgart: Klett-Cotta, Helsinki: Otava.
Mit Beiträgen und Gedichten von sámischen AutorInnen: Samuli Aikio, Leena Morottaja, Veli-Pekka Lehtola, Paulus Utsi, Nils Mathis Vars und Kirsti Paltto.

Kasten, Erich 1983. Kulturwandel bei den Samen. Eine ethno-historische Untersuchung zum Kulturkontakt in Schwedisch-Lappland. Berlin: Dietrich Reimer Verlag. (Dissertation, Ethnologie, Freie Universität Berlin)

Linné, Carl von 1975 [1964]. Lappländische Reise. Übersetzt von H. C. Artmann. Frankfurt: Insel Verlag.

Lüderwaldt, Andreas 1976. Joiken aus Norwegen. Studien zur Charakteristik und gesellschaftlichen Bedeutung des lappischen Gesanges. Veröffentlichungen aus dem Übersee-Museum Bremen, Reihe D, Band 2. Bremen: Übersee-Museum.

Manker, Ernst 1964. Volk der acht Jahreszeiten. Das große Lapplandbuch. München: BLV-Verlag.

Mann, Klaus 1981 [1934, 1977]. Flucht in den Norden. Hamburg: Rowohlt.

Müller-Wille, Ludger 1974. Lappen und Finnen in Utsjoki (Ohcijohka), Finnland. (Westfälische Geographische Studien 30). Münster: Institut für Geographie und Länderkunde und Geographische Kommission für Westfalen. (Dissertation, Ethnologie, Münster)

Sápmi. Zeitschrift der Lappland-Initiative Bremen e. V. Erstausgabe 1/2001. Adresse: M. & G. Böttcher, Wulfhoopstrasse 41, D-28201 Bremen.

Schefferus, Joannis 1675. Lappland / Das ist: Neue und wahrhafftige Beschreibung von Lappland und dessen Einwohnern... Frankfurt: Martin Hallervorden.

Schneider, Lothar (Hsg.) 2001. Lappland. Kärnten: Wieser-Verlag. (unter anderem Übersetzungen von sámischer Literatur).

Schwaar, Hans Ueli 1991. Nordland. Lieder, Joik, Samen und Gedichte aus Lappland. Frauenfeld: Im Waldgut.

Schwaar, Hans Ueli 1994. Am Rande der Arktis. Abenteuer Lappland - Natur, Rentier, Samen, Touristen und die neue Zeit. Frauenfeld: Im Waldgut.

Schwaar, Hans Ueli 1996. Sapmi. Mythen und Sagen der Samen und ihr religiöser Hintergrund. Frauenfeld: Im Waldgut.

Schwaar, Hans Ueli 1999. Näkkälä. Jeden Tag, ein Jahr. 360 Aufzeichnungen aus Lappland. Frauenfeld: Im Waldgut.

Schwaar, Hans Ueli 2000. Tundra, Sumpf und Birkenduft. Leben mit den Samen in Lappland. Frauenfeld: Im Waldgut.

Seiwert, W. D. 2000. Die Saami - Indigenes Volk am Anfang Europas. Leipzig.

Tuomi-Nikula, Outi 2001. Sápmi, das Land der Fischer, Jäger und Rentierzüchter. Schleswig, Schloss Gottorp: Verein zur Förderung des Archäologischen Landesmuseum.

Vorren, Ørnulv und Ernst Manker 1967. Die Lappen. Übersetzung von Hanna Köster-Ljung und Bernd G. Balke. Braunschweig: Westermann-Verlag.

Wustmann, Erich 1971. 1000 Meilen im Rentierschlitten. Ein Leben in der Wildmark. Radebeul: Neumann Verlag.

Littérature en français

Arthaud, Jacques 1956. Derniers nomades du Grand Nord. Ces hommes de 30.000 ans. Paris: Arthaud.

Fernandez, M. M. Jocelyne 1982. Le finnois parlé par les Sames bilingues d'Utsjoki-Ohcejohka (Laponie finlandaise) - Structures constratives, syntaxiques et discursives. (L'Europe de Tradition Orale 1). Paris: Société d'Études Linguistiques et Anthropologiques de France.

Gabus, Jean 1939. Sous les tentes lapones. Neuchâtel: Attinger.

Gourmont, Remy de 1890. Chez les Lapons. Moeurs, Coutumes et Légendes de la Laponie norvégienne. Paris: F. Didot.

Mériot, Christian 1980. Le Lapons et leur société. (Études d'ethnologie historique). Toulouse: Édouard Privat.

Scheffer, Johannes 1678. Histoire de la Laponie. Paris.

INDEX

Note: Page numbers in *italics* refer to illustrations.